Intermittent Fasting Diet for Women

For Weight loss after 50 years

Author

Pauline D. Madrid

Contents

19. Healthy Frittata w/ Scallions & Smoked Salmon
20. Chocolate Peanut Butter Milkshake

HEALTHY INTERMITTENT LUNCH RECIPES

21. Satisfying Grilled Mushrooms
22. Superfood Detox & Cleanse Salad
23. Satisfying Turkey Lettuce Wraps
24. Beautiful Berry Salad with Citrus-Strawberry Dressing
25. Mung-Spinach Cleansing Soup
26. Broccoli Slaw with Pineapple Curry Dressing
27. Collard Wraps with Satay Dipping Sauce
28. Fried Tofu w/ Tender Spring Greens
29. Healthy Green Bean & Zucchini Sauté
30. Master Cleanse Salad
31. Raw Spicy Zoodle Bowl
32. Citrus Raw Kale Avocado Salad
33. Mixed Green & Salmon Salad with Toasted Walnuts
34. Garden Salad with Lemony Dressing
35. Blueberry Pineapple Salad with Citrus Chia Seed Dressing
36. Healthy Vegetable Sauté
37. Arugula, Avocado, & Orange Salad
38. Healthy Cauliflower Cream Dill Soup
39. Fat-Burning Spinach & Beet Salad
40. Citric Spinach Salad

HEALTHY INTERMITTENT DINNER RECIPES

41. Lean Steak with Oregano-Orange Chimichurri & Arugula Salad
42. Steamed Bass with Fennel, Parsley, and Capers
43. Crunchy Chicken w/ Mustard-Orange Vinaigrette Dressing
44. Pan-Seared Salmon Salad with Snow Peas & Grapefruit
45. Stir-Fried Chicken with Water Chestnuts
46. Roasted Shrimp & Broccoli
47. Sweet & Sour Chicken with Mixed Greens
48. Steamed Salmon w/ Fennel & Fresh Herbs
49. Tangerine Ham with Baby Carrots
50. Lemon Garlic Salmon

51. Perfect Grilled Pork Roast Served with Fruit Compote
52. Mango Chili Chicken Stir Fry
53. Tasty Sesame Salmon
54. Veggie & Beef Salad Bowl
55. Baked Salmon with Dill-Avocado Yogurt
56. Crock Pot Coconut Curry Shrimp
57. Delicious Baked Tilapia in Garlic & Olive Oil
58. Turkey w/ Capers, Tomatoes, and Greens Beans
59. Grilled Tuna w/ Bean & Tomato Salad
60. Teriyaki Fish w/ Zucchini

HEALTHY INTERMITTENT SNACKS/DESSERTS

61. Grain-Free Mixed Seed Crackers
62. Citrus Avocado Snack
63. Apricots & Walnuts Snack
64. Anti-Inflammatory Trail Mix
65. Crispy Lemon- Chili Roasted Kale
66. Citrus Greek Yogurt
67. Curried Cashews
68. Spicy Yogurt Dip with Veggies
69. Bell Pepper Candies
70. Veggies with Almond-Butter Dip
71. Warm Lemon Rosemary Olives
72. Creamy Cucumbers
73. Vinegar & Salt Kale Chips
74. Healthy Stuffed Mushrooms 75. Squash Fries
76. Delicious Ginger Tahini Dip
77. Carrot French Fries
78. Candied Macadamia Nuts
79. Healthy Pistachio & Dark Chocolate Kiwi
80. Spicy Peanut Masala

HEALTHY INTERMITTENT DRINKS

81. Chilled Ginger Lemon Pomegranate Juice
82. Chilled Metabolism Detox Drink
83. Delicious Strawberry Punch

Introduction

For the longest of time, many of us believed that breakfast is the most important meal of the day. But, turns out skipping your favorite bowl of oats with a side of fruit does more good than harm. While intermittent fasting may seem like a new type of diet, it is perhaps one of the oldest lifestyles.

If we go back to the hunter-gatherer era where the next meal wasn't guaranteed, our ancestors would mostly eat one or two meals a day. If we also look at traditional Ayurveda and Chinese medicine, they advocate for regular fasts as a way of promoting general wellness and mental clarity. Fasting is also very common in some religions for spiritual as well as physical benefits.

Understanding Intermittent Fasting (IF)

Intermittent fasting describes an interval of time where you do not eat or drink. Water, coffee and tea with no sugar or sweetener and bone broth are however allowed during the fasting period. An important point to note is that intermittent fasting is by no way similar to a calorie restrictive diet or starvation as it simply reduces your eating time window. A better way to describe intermittent fasting is that it is a pattern of eating and not a diet.

With easy access to food for most people, we have programmed our bodies to expect food three to six times in a day, not including mindless munching on our favorite snacks. What intermittent fasting dos is to reduce your eating window to help your body take a break from the digestion process, that utilizes quite a lot of energy, and focus on other bodily functions that are just as important. These are processes such as immune boosting, cellular repair, gaining mental reducing oxidative stress caused by free radicals.

Types of Intermittent Fasting

- Time-restricted Fasting

The most popular form of time-restricted fasting involves abstinence from food for a period of 12 to 16 hours and eating for 12 to 8 hours, respectively. However, once you become super comfortable with maybe fasting for 16 hours and only eating in an 8 hour window, you may find yourself pushing the fasting hours to 18 and even 20 hours, thus reducing your eating time window to 6 and 4 hours respectively. An important point to note is there's no restriction for what you can eat in the eating time window.

- 5-2

This type of intermittent fasting involves eating as you normally would for 5 days and fasting for 2 days, consecutive or non-consecutive with a calorie restriction of 500-600 calories for the two fast days.

- Alternate day fasting

This involves alternate days of eating and fasting. So, if you eat today, you fast for the next 24 hours and so on.

Intermittent Fasting For Women Over 50

Two of the biggest challenges for women over 50 is weight loss and a hormonal system that's out of whack. Difficulty in weight loss can be attributed to a slower metabolism, significantly lower muscle mass, uneven sleep pattern and aching joints. A hormone system that's out of whack can be attributed to the onset of menopause and an uneven sleep pattern.

As you grow older, the risk of disease also increases especially if you can't seem to get rid of belly fat, as this surrounds your most vital organs. Intermittent fasting is a great way to boost metabolism and weight loss. Additionally it promotes longevity as the body is able to focus on other important functions such as normalizing the hormone system, cellular repair and boosting cognitive function aside from digestion. This goes a long way in reducing the chance of developing the typical age-related disease.

The science behind Intermittent Fasting

When you eat, your brain triggers the pancreas to produce insulin which it uses to store glucose from the carbs you consumed, for later use. With the ready availability of food and eating about 3-6 times a day, your body finds itself in a situation where it is storing more food than it is using for energy, putting your body in an anabolic state.

When glucose is stored in your body, it is stored as fat and with constant storing, you start noticing yourself gaining weight. What intermittent fasting does is to reverse this process of fat storage by triggering your cells to release the stored fat and use it for energy, especially during the fasting window. This process is referred to as a catabolic state, which simply means to break down and with continued intermittent fasting, you start noticing weight loss.

HGH (Human Growth Hormone) is released in response to your boy's need for glucose during the fasting window. This hormone is essential for boosting your metabolism, fat burning and muscle repair. When you eat in very regular intervals, 3 to 6, through the day, the production of HGH is suppressed and you start having a sluggish metabolism and you start piling on the pounds.

Noradrenaline is another hormone that is released when you are on an empty stomach. It is a signal sent out by your nervous system instructing your cells to release stored fat for fuel.

Intermittent fasting and Autophagy

Autophagy comes from Greek and literally means self-eating, auto-self and phagein-to eat. Autophagy is the process of your body eliminating broken down cells as well as all old cell components which include cell membranes, organelles and protein. This process helps your body to recycle all your cellular components.

In lay man's terms, autophagy is simply replacing the old and worn out parts of cells in your body. We can compare this to a car that you have had for a while. Servicing your car involves replacing worn our parts of the car for it to function really well and you will notice that if you regularly service your car, as advised, then it keeps running like new. The case is the same for our bodies. We need to service them on a regular basis for longevity.

So, what triggers the process of autophagy?

Nutrient deprivation. Remember the hormone insulin that is released when you eat to help store carbs as glucose in your body for a rainy day? Well, there exists another hormone, glucagon that acts opposite of insulin. So when your insulin levels are high, your glucagon levels are low and vice versa.

The fasting window in intermittent fasting causes insulin levels to drop and the glucagon levels to rise which activates the autophagy process. So by practicing intermittent fasting, your body benefits from cellular repair by eliminating all junky parts of your cells and also from the production of the Human Growth Hormone that stimulates the production of new cell parts.

Considerations to make when intermittent fasting for women over 50

- Be flexible

The great thing about IF is that it's not cut and stone, it's your design. Start slow by doing a 12 hour fast followed by a 12 hour eating window. Once you are comfortable with this, increase your fasting window to 14, 16, and 18 subsequently. Once in a while you will find it difficult to fast for 18 hours, if you had already reached this stage, and it's okay to fall back to 16 or 14 hours then start building up again. You can also try alternate day fasting or the 5-2 to see which works best for you.

- Rewire your way of thinking

At first mention, people interpret fasting as deprivation which is not true. People who practice intermittent fasting actually find that they have more time on their hands as they don't have to think about what to make for breakfast. Once you rewire your thought process towards fasting, you will actually be more open to tray it.

- Being busy is a great distraction

We have already established that IF actually frees some of the time you would have used meal prepping 3-5 meals in a day. Another great consideration is that the busier you are, the faster the fasting window is going to elapse. Try to busy yourself during the fasting window so you don't find yourself counting down the time to your eating window second by second.

- Exercise for maximum benefit

One thing about exercising and IF that seems crazy is that you will notice that your hunger actually reduces when you are exercising. Additionally, the increased metabolism from both fasting and exercising helps you lose weight, improve your skin's glow, improve digestion even faster.

- Sleep for 7-8 hours for best results

During your sleep is the time your body actually repairs itself and replenishes your used up energy in readiness for the next day. You will realize when you get enough sleep, the fasting window is not going to be difficult. Sleeping for few hours on the other hand will activate the hunger hormone – ghrelin, as your body will be signaling you to eat more for energy now that your body was not able to reenergize naturally. This will make fasting really difficult as you'll be experiencing the craziest cravings.

- Give yourself time to discover the best IF method for you

As mentioned earlier, don't be in a hurry to dive deep into an 18-6 fast. Prepare your body by starting slow and also trying the different methods to see which is actually perfect for you and which you can carry on with forever. Remember, IF is a lifestyle and not a quick fix.

- Break your fast with fresh and natural food products

In as much as IF is not restrictive, you want to get the best out of it. Consider the fact that you will have stayed for a significant amount of time without food and your body will be ready for it. You therefore want to break your fast with food that will actually provide your body with the nutrition it needs to help flush out the worn out cell parts that have been discarded. teach yourself to not be an overcompensate who feels that because you have been fasting for the last 16 hours then you need to reward yourself with the biggest slice of cake.

Start fresh and natural and 3-4 hours in you can have some cake. Chances are you won't even be craving for it!

- Hydrate, hydrate and hydrate

Water is going to be your best friend when you are on IF as this will help you flush out toxins and old cells and also help stave off hunger.

- Aim for a natural balanced diet

We are aiming for longevity and hand in hand with IF and exercise is a natural balanced diet. This will provide your cells with healthy nutrition and also help run all your bodily functions. You want to avoid processed foods that don't actually offer any nutrition and that carry a lot of chemicals that can actually cause illnesses such as cancer.

Managing Your Food Intake

Truth be told, adapting to intermittent fasting is not the easiest thing especially if you were used to taking 5-6 regular meals every day. The first thing you will notice is that you will be tempted to binge on anything that is edible that is at your disposal when breaking your fast. However, to avoid this happening to you, you should prep your meals in advance and not when you on the fasting window, at least when you are still an IF rookie as this temptation can be quite unbearable.

Prep some fruit and veggies to take as your first meal, preferably a smoothie then for your second meal introduce some protein and a few whole carbs If you still have room for a third meal, it should have more veggies and fruit than protein and carbs. You will notice that our recipe section has very simple and tasty meals prepared from natural foods, which is what you need when intermittent fasting.

Before you embark on intermittent fasting, start by cleaning up your eating habits. What does this mean? Get rid of super processed foods and replace these with healthy and natural foods. Fill up on fruit, vegetable, whole carbs such as whole wheat, quinoa, bulgur, lentils, grains, pulses and nuts. Do this for a whole week. For meats aim to get wild caught fish, grass fed beef, free range poultry, hormone free pork and so on. For every food choice, go with the healthiest.

Exercising safely with Intermittent Fasting

Intermittent fasting and working out go hand in hand and you stand to gain more benefits by doing the two. However, you need to consider the following for you to get in an effective workout session when fasting.

- Work on your timing

When fasting, you can either exercise before, during or after your eating window and this boils down to preference. Do you prefer working out on an empty stomach? Then working out about an hour to the end of your fast might work perfectly for you. Some people find it easier to exercise after their first light meal such as a smoothie or waiting until the end of the eating window to exercise. To be honest, to know which works best for you will require some trial and error on your part.

- Choose your exercise for the day based on your macronutrients

Different exercises require different amounts of energy. For example, strength workouts would require more energy than cycling. On the day before you should know tomorrow's exercise so you are able to feed appropriately. For example, on the day before strength training you can consume more whole carbs than you normally would.

- Eat the right food after your workout for maximum results

Protein and vegetables are very important after a workout as these help refuel your body and also support muscle growth and repair. You can also add in a few whole carbs to help boost your energy levels. The rule of thumb is to eat whole natural foods after a workout session.

- Drink up!

Hydrating is very important when exercising, more so when you are fasting. This will help you stay a tad more energetic and also help replenish the water you lose when sweating.

- Keep the exercise period and duration moderate

This is especially true when you are in the beginner level. Going too hard will cause you to get dizzy and not as productive. Aim for 20-30 minute workouts that are not extremely tasking especially for a start. Then, as you get more and more in tune with intermittent fasting, you can moderately increase the intensity of your workouts, within reason.

Now that we have all the basics of intermittent fasting covered, let's now get to our tasty recipes that are specially designed for intermittent fasting. Enjoy!

INTERMITTENT DIET BREAKFAST RECIPES

1. Healthy Rainbow Acai Bowl

Yield: 2 Servings
Total Time: 5 Minutes
Prep Time: 5 Minutes
Cook Time: N/A

Ingredients

- 1/4 cup frozen raspberries
- 1/4 cup frozen blueberries
- 1/2 cup nonfat Greek yoghurt
- 1 teaspoon chia seeds
- 1 teaspoon acai powder
- 1 teaspoon vanilla protein powder
- 1 mango, sliced
- 1 small orange, segmented
- 1 tablespoon pistachios, chopped, toasted

Directions

In a blender, blend together, berries, yogurt, chia seed, acai powder, and mango until very smooth; spoon into two serving bowls and top each with fresh blueberries, strawberries, banana, orange and pistachios. Enjoy!

Nutrition info Per Serving:

Calories: 198; Total Fat: 2.9 g; Carbs: 11.5 g; Dietary Fiber: 6.4 g; Sugars: 6.6; Protein: 18.6 g; Cholesterol: 3 mg; Sodium: 31 mg

Yield: 1 Serving

2. Yummy Breakfast Stir Fry

Total Time: 50 Minutes
Prep Time: 10 Minutes
Cook Time: 40 Minutes

Ingredients

- 4 egg whites, beaten
- 2 small onions, chopped
- 1   green pepper, chopped
- 2   medium tomatoes, chopped
- A handful mushrooms, chopped
- ½ tablespoon extra-virgin olive oil,
- A pinch of sea salt
- Black olives, hot banana peppers and sliced cucumber, for serving

Directions

Add olive oil to a pan and add the green peppers. Cover and cook on high heat for about 2 minutes then lower the heat and cook for 3 more minutes.

Next add the onions and the mushrooms and cover. Cook until tender then stir in the tomatoes. Sprinkle the salt, cover and simmer for about 15 minutes or until the melamen is soft and juicy.

Gently drizzle the egg whites over the melamen. Allow to cook without stirring for about a minute.

Roast the hot bananas peppers on your burner over medium heat, careful not burn them too much.

Serve the stir fry with whole wheat pita bread, black olives, roasted hot banana pepper and sliced cucumbers. You can also serve with traditional Mediterranean tea.

Enjoy!

Nutritional Information Per Serving:

Calories: 330; Total Fat: 9.3 g; Carbs: 17.4 g; Dietary Fiber: 13.1 g; Sugars: 3.7 g; Protein: 22.9 g; Cholesterol: 0 mg; Sodium: 209 mg

Yield: 1 Serving

3. Whole Grain Breakfast Wraps

Total Time: 50 Minutes
Prep Time: 10 Minutes
Cook Time: 40 Minutes

Ingredients

- 2   whole grain flax wraps
- 3   egg whites
- 1 ½ tbsp. extra virgin olive oil
- ¼ cup sun dried tomatoes
- ¼ cup fresh spinach, chopped
- ¼ cup crumbled feta cheese
- Sea salt and freshly ground pepper to taste

Directions

Heat the oil in a nonstick pan and sauté the tomatoes, spinach and egg whites until almost done then flip and cook the other side.

Add the crumbled feta to warm it up. Sprinkle with salt and pepper then remove from heat.

Heat the wraps on a dry pan then serve the egg mixture into the wraps and roll them up. Enjoy!

Nutritional Information Per Serving:

Calories: 391; Total Fat: 33.1 g; Carbs: 17.4 g; Dietary Fiber: 1.8 g; Sugars: 2.3 g; Protein: 17.7 g; Cholesterol: 33 mg; Sodium: 529 mg

4. Cranberry Detox Smoothie

Yield: 3 Servings
Total Time: 5 Minutes
Prep Time: 5 Minutes
Cook Time: N/A

Ingredients

- 1 cup frozen cranberries
- 1 cup blueberries
- 1 apple, diced
- 1 cup almond milk
- 1/2 teaspoon ground turmeric
- 1/2 teaspoon ground cinnamon

Directions

In a blender, blend together apple, cranberries, blueberries, and almond milk until very smooth. Serve in a tall glass garnished with ground turmeric and cinnamon. Enjoy!

Nutritional Information per Serving:
Calories: 273; Total Fat: 19.4 g; Carbs: 25.6 g; Dietary Fiber: 6.3 g; Sugars: 16.6 g; Protein: 2.5 g; Cholesterol: 0 mg; Sodium: 13 mg

5. Red Pepper & Smoked Salmon Scramble

Total Time: 15Minutes
Prep Time: 10 Minutes
Cook Time: 5 Minutes

Ingredients

Yield: 1 Serving

- 2 whole eggs and 1 egg yolk
- ⅛ teaspoon garlic powder
- 1   tablespoon chopped fresh dill
- 2   pieces smoked salmon, torn apart
- ⅛ teaspoon red pepper flakes
- Salt and pepper
- 1 tablespoon extra-virgin olive oil

Directions

Beat the eggs in a bowl; stir in garlic, dill, salmon, red pepper flakes, black pepper and salt until well combined.

Set a saucepan over low heat; add extra virgin olive oil. Once warm, add the egg mixture and cook, stirring until cooked through. Serve topped with roasted veggies.

Nutritional Information per Serving:

Calories: 376; Total Fat: 29.9 g; Carbs: 3.5 g; Dietary Fiber: 0.5 g; Protein: 24.9 g; Cholesterol: 550 mg; Sodium: 1272 mg; Sugars: 0.9 g

6. Cinnamon Berry Shake

Yield: 4 Servings
Total Time: 5 Minutes
Prep Time: 5 Minutes
Cook Time: N/A

Ingredients

- ½ cup blackberries
- ½ cup blueberries
- ½ cup raspberries
- 2 cups coconut milk
- / avocado
- 1 teaspoon cinnamon
- 1 teaspoon liquid stevia
- 2 tablespoons almond butter

Directions

Blend everything together until very smooth. Enjoy!

Nutritional Information per Serving:

Calories: 378; Total Fat: 35.8 g; Carbs: 5.9 g; Dietary Fiber: 7 g; Sugars: 7.8 g; Protein: 5.3 g; Cholesterol: 0 mg; Sodium: 20 mg

7. Nutty Blueberry Detox Porridge

Yield: 4 Servings
Total Time: 12 Minutes
Prep Time: 5 Minutes
Cook Time: 7 Minutes

Ingredients

- 1 cup almond milk
- 1 cup rolled oats
- 1 cup blueberries
- 1 teaspoon coconut oil
- 3 teaspoons raw honey
- 1 peach, thinly sliced
- Mixed nuts and seeds (hazelnuts, sunflower seeds, sesame seeds and chia seeds)

Directions

Combine milk and oats in a small pan set over medium heat; bring to a gentle boil. Simmer for about 5 minutes, stirring frequently; transfer the mixture to a blender and add in berries, coconut oil and raw honey; blend until very smooth.

Ladle porridge into serving bowls and top each with peach slices, mixed seeds and nuts and extra raw honey. Enjoy! **Nutritional Information per Serving:**

Calories: 277; Total Fat: 17 g; Carbs: 30.2 g; Dietary Fiber: 4.9 g; Sugars: 23.6 g; Protein: 4.7 g; Cholesterol: 0 mg; Sodium: 11 mg

8. Superfood Detox Parfait

Yield: 1 Serving
Total Time: 5 Minutes
Prep Time: 5 Minutes

Cook Time: 5 Minutes

Ingredients

- 1/4 cup Greek yogurt
- ¼ cup granola cereal
- 1/4 cup blueberry compote
- 1/4 cup trail mix
- 1 teaspoon ground flax 1
  teaspoon chia seeds

Directions

Layer the ingredients in a glass according to your preference; stir and eat!
Nutritional Information per Serving:

Calories: 232; Total Fat: 2.4 g; Carbs: 33.4 g; Dietary Fiber: 4.8 g; Sugars: 11 g; Protein: 13.9 g; Cholesterol: 0 mg; Sodium: 98 mg

9. Berry Acai Lucuma Breakfast Bowl

Yield: 3 Servings
Total Time: 5 Minutes
Prep Time: 5 Minutes Cook
Time: 5 Minutes

Ingredients:

- ½ cup blueberries
- ½ cup blackberries
- ½ cup raspberries
- ½ cup goji berries
- 2 tablespoons acai powder
- 1 teaspoon lucuma powder
- 1/2 avocado
- 1/2 frozen banana
- ½ cup diced mango
- 1/2 cup almond milk

Handful blueberries and chia seeds, for topping

Directions:

In a blender, blend all ingredients until very smooth. Serve topped with chia seeds and blueberries. Enjoy!

Nutritional Information per Serving:

Calories: 413; Total Fat: 26.8 g; Carbs: 45.6 g; Dietary Fiber: 12.5 g; Sugars: 28.1 g; Protein: 4.7 g; Cholesterol: 0 mg; Sodium: 19 mg

10. Delicious Breakfast Turkey Casserole

Yield: 6 Servings
Total Time: 50 Minutes
Prep Time: 5 Minutes
Cook Time: 45 Minutes

Ingredients

- 1 tablespoon coconut oil
- 1/2 pound ground turkey
- 1 large sweet potato, cut into slices
- 1/2 cup spinach
- 12 eggs
- Salt and pepper

Directions

Preheat oven to 350°F. Lightly coat a square baking tray with coconut oil and set aside.

In a skillet set over medium heat, brown ground turkey in coconut oil; season well and remove from heat.

Layer the potato slices onto the baking tray and top with raw spinach and ground turkey.

In a small bowl, whisk eggs, salt and pepper until well blended; pour over the mixture to cover completely; bake for about 45 minutes or until eggs are cooked through and the potatoes are tender. Remove from oven and let cool a bit before serving.

Nutrition info Per Serving:

Calories: 247; Total Fat: 15.2 g; Carbs: 7 g; Dietary Fiber: 1.1 g; Sugars: 2.6; Protein: 22.1 g; Cholesterol: 366 mg; Sodium: 176 mg

11. Fruity Parfait

Yield: 2 Servings

Total Time: 10 Minutes

Prep Time: 10 Minutes

Cook Time: N/A

Ingredients

- 1 cup nonfat Greek yogurt
- ½ banana, sliced
- 1   cup mixed berries
- 2   tablespoons crunchy whole-grain cereal1 tablespoon
- flaxseed

Directions

In a tall serving glass, alternate the layers of nonfat Greek yogurt, banana slice, and mixed berries. Top with crunchy whole grain cereal and flaxseed. Enjoy!

Nutritional Information per Serving:

Calories: 182; Total Fat: 3.8 g; Carbs: 23.7 g; Dietary Fiber: 4.7 g; Sugars: 14.5 g; Protein: 13.2 g; Cholesterol: 6 mg; Sodium: 53 mg

12. Fat-Burning Overnight Oats

Yield: 2 Servings
Total Time: 10 Minutes + Chilling Time
Prep Time: 10 Minutes
Cook Time: N/A

Ingredients

- 1/2 cup oats
- 1 teaspoon chia seeds
- 1/2 cup vanilla almond milk (unsweetened)
- 1/4 cup fresh blueberries
- 1/4 banana, chopped
- 1/4 cup chopped fresh pineapple
- 1/4 cup nonfat Greek yogurt
- 1/4 teaspoon cinnamon

1 tablespoon chopped almonds

Directions

In a small jar, combine oats, chia seeds, almond milk, blueberries, banana, pineapple, yogurt, cinnamon and chopped almonds. Refrigerate overnight.

To serve, remove from the fridge and stir to mix well before serving.

Nutritional Information per Serving:

Calories: 310; Total Fat: 18.4 g; Carbs: 29 g; Dietary Fiber: 5 g; Protein: 10.8 g; Cholesterol: 3 mg; Sodium: 29 mg; Sugars: 10.2 g

13. Tasty Berry Omelet

Yield: 1 Serving
Total Time: 17 Minutes
Prep Time: 10 Minutes
Cook Time: 7 Minutes

Ingredients

- 1 large egg
- 1 tablespoon almond milk
- ¼ teaspoon cinnamon
- ½ teaspoon rapeseed oil
- 100g cottage cheese
- 1 ½ cups chopped raspberries, blueberries, and strawberries

Directions

In a bowl, beat together the egg, milk and cinnamon until well blended.

Add oil to a nonstick pan set over medium heat. Add the egg mixture and swirl to cover the base evenly. Cook the egg mixture until set.

Transfer the omelet to a plate and sprinkle with cheese. Top with berries and roll up to serve.

Nutritional Information per Serving:

Calories: 298; Total Fat: 12.2 g; Carbs: 26.2 g; Dietary Fiber: 12 g; Protein: 22.5 g; Cholesterol: 149 mg; Sodium: 480 mg; Sugars: 9 g

14. Healthy Tomato-Garlic Toasts

Yield: 1 Serving
Total Time: 20 Minutes
Prep Time: 15 Minutes
Cook Time: 5 Minutes

Ingredients

- 2 slices whole-wheat bread
- 1 small clove garlic, cut in half
- 1/2 teaspoon extra-virgin olive oil
- 1 small plum tomato, cut in half
- Kosher salt
- Pepper

Directions

Toast or grill the bread. Rub one side of the grilled or toasted bread with garlic and drizzle with olive oil. Rub with tomato and sprinkle with pepper and salt. Enjoy!

Nutritional Information per Serving:

Calories: 162; Total Fat: 4.2 g; Carbs: 25.2 g; Dietary Fiber: 3.8 g; Protein: 7.3 g; Cholesterol: 0 mg; Sodium: 419 mg; Sugars: 3.1 g

15. Sausage & Broccoli Breakfast Quiche

Yield: 8 Servings
Total Time: 1 Hour 10 Minutes
Prep Time: 15 Minutes
Cook Time: 55 Minutes

Ingredients

- 1   cup broccoli
- ½ pound breakfast sausage
- 2   cups almond flour
- 1 tablespoon sea salt
- 9 eggs
- 2 tablespoons coconut oil 2 tablespoons water

Directions

Steam the broccoli and set aside.
Cook the sausage and set aside.
Blend almond flour and sea salt in a food processor until well combined.
Add one egg and coconut oil and continue processing to form a ball.
Spread the dough on a quiche dish and top with broccoli and sausage.
In a bowl, whisk the remaining eggs with water and pour over the broccoli and sausage.
Bake at 350°Ffor about 35 minutes or until firm and cooked through.

Nutritional Information per Serving:

Calories: 338; Total Fat: 23.8 g; Carbs: 6.2 g; Dietary Fiber: 3.3 g; Protein: 17.6 g; Cholesterol: 208 mg; Sodium: 520 mg; Sugars: 1.6 g

16. Breakfast Pumpkin Granola

Yield: 8 Servings
Total Time: 15Minutes
Prep Time: 10 Minutes
Cook Time: 5 Minutes

Ingredients

- ½ cup chopped dates
- 1 cup almond meal
- 1½ cup chopped coconut flakes
- 1 cup pumpkin seeds
- 1 cup dried cranberries
- 1 cup pecans, chopped
- 1½ cup sliced almonds
- 1 teaspoon cinnamon
- ½ cup coconut oil
- 1 teaspoon pumpkin pie spice ½ cup pumpkin puree

Directions

Preheat your oven to 275°F. Line baking sheet with parchment paper.

Combine together dates, almond flour, coconut flakes, pumpkin seeds, cranberries, pecans almonds and cinnamon in a bowl.

Stir in the wet ingredients until well combined.

Spread the mixture on the baking sheet and bake for about 1 hour, stirring after every 15 minutes.

Nutritional Information per Serving:

Calories: 493; Total Fat: 42.8 g; Carbs: 23.2 g; Dietary Fiber: 7.9 g; Protein: 11.7 g; Cholesterol: 0 mg; Sodium: 8 mg; Sugars: 10.5 g

Yield: 24 servings (1/3 cup per serving)
Total Time: 45 Minutes
Prep Time: 10 Minutes
Cook Time: 30 Minutes

Ingredients

- 7 ounces chopped dried mixed fruit
- 1/4 teaspoon ground nutmeg
- 1 teaspoon ground cinnamon
- 1/2 cup wheat germ
- 3/4 cup chopped walnuts
- 1 cup quick-cooking barley
- 4 1/2 cups oats
- 1 1/2 tablespoons vanilla extract
- 3 tablespoons canola oil
- 1/3 cup honey
- 1/2 cup maple syrup Cooking spray

Directions

Preheat your oven to 325F°.

In a bowl, whisk the wet ingredients until well blended.

In a separate bowl, combine the dry ingredients. Stir in wet mixture and spread the mixture onto a pan. Bake, stirring every 10 minutes, for about 30 minutes or until browned.

Stir in the dried fruit and let cool completely before serving.

Nutritional Information per Serving:

Calories: 163; Total Fat: 5.4 g; Carbs: 25.6 g; Dietary Fiber: 2.8 g; Protein: 4.2 g; Cholesterol: 0 mg; Sodium: 2 mg; Sugars: 8.3 g

18. Low-Fat Dill-Tomato Frittata

Yield: 4 Servings
Total Time: 45 Minutes
Prep Time: 10 Minutes
Cook Time: 30 Minutes

Ingredients

- 8 eggs, whisked
- Coconut oil to grease pan
- 4 tomatoes, diced
- 1   teaspoon red pepper flakes
- 2   garlic cloves, minced
- 2 tablespoons chopped fresh chives
- 2 tablespoons chopped fresh dill Salt and pepper

Directions

Preheat your oven to 325°F.

Spray a cast iron skillet or saucepan with olive oil spray.

In a bowl, whisk together eggs and the remaining ingredients until well blended.

Pour the mixture into the pan and bake for about 30 minutes or until cooked through. To serve, garnish with extra chives and dill.

Nutritional Information per Serving:

Calories: 157; Total Fat: 10.2 g; Carbs: 7.2 g; Dietary Fiber: 1.9 g; Protein: 12.7 g; Cholesterol: 327 mg; Sodium: 133 mg; Sugars: 4 g

19. Healthy Frittata w/ Scallions & Smoked Salmon

Yield: 6 servings

Total Time: 30 Minutes
Prep Time: 10 Minutes
Cook Time: 20 Minutes

Ingredients

- 2 teaspoons extra-virgin olive oil
- 6 scallions, trimmed and chopped
- 4 large eggs
- 6 large egg whites
- ½ teaspoon finely chopped fresh tarragon
- ¼ cup water
- ½ teaspoon salt
- 2 ounces smoked salmon, sliced into small pieces 2 tablespoons black olive tapenade

Directions

Preheat your oven to 350°F.

Set a large ovenproof pan over medium heat; add oil and heat until hot, but not smoky. Stir in scallions and sauté, stirring, for about 3 minutes or until tender and fragrant.

In a bowl, beat together eggs, egg whites, tarragon, water, and salt; season with black pepper and pour into the pan. Arrange the salmon onto the egg mixture. Cook, stirring frequently, for about 2 minutes or until almost set; transfer to the oven and cook for about 14 minutes or until puffed and golden. Remove the frittata from the oven and transfer to a serving plate; slice and serve with tapenade.

Nutritional Information per Serving:

Calories: 186; Total Fat: 5 g; Carbs: 1 g; Dietary Fiber: trace; Protein: 10 g; Cholesterol: 143 mg; Sodium: 535 mg; Sugars: trace

20. Chocolate Peanut Butter Milkshake

Yield: 1 Serving
Total Time: 5 Minutes
Prep Time: 5 Minutes
Cook Time: N/A

Ingredients

- 1 tablespoon natural peanut butter
- 1 tablespoon unsweetened cocoa powder
- 1 cup unsweetened coconut milk
- Pinch of sea salt
- 1 teaspoon liquid stevia 1
- scoop protein powder

Directions

Blend all ingredients together until smooth. Enjoy!

Nutritional Information per Serving:

Calories: 664; Total Fat: 66 g; Carbs: 19.2 g; Dietary Fiber: 8.1 g; Sugars: 9.1 g; Protein: 31.6 g; Cholesterol: 0 mg; Sodium: 274 mg

21. Satisfying Grilled Mushrooms

Yield: 4 Servings
Total Time: 20 Minutes
Prep Time: 10 Minutes
Cook Time: 10 Minutes

Ingredients

- 2 cups shiitake mushrooms
- 1   tablespoon balsamic vinegar
- 1/4 cup extra virgin olive oil
- 1-2 garlic cloves, minced
- A handful of parsley 1
- teaspoon salt

Directions

Rinse the mushroom and pat dry; put in a foil and drizzle with balsamic vinegar and extra virgin olive oil.

Sprinkle the mushroom with garlic, parsley, and salt.

Grill for about 10 minutes or until tender and cooked through. Serve warm.

Nutritional Information per Serving:

Calories: 171; Total Fat: 12.8g; Carbs: 15.9g; Dietary Fiber: 2.4g; Protein: 1.8g; Cholesterol: 0mg; Sodium: 854mg; sugars: 4.1g

22. Superfood Detox & Cleanse Salad

Yields: 4 Servings

Total Time: 10 Minutes
Prep Time: 10 Minutes
Cook Time: N/A

Ingredients

- 1 cup fresh blueberries
- 1 cup shredded carrots
- 5 cups baby spinach
- 12 raw almonds, sliced
- 2 dates, pitted and diced
- 1   tablespoon fresh lemon juice
- 2   tablespoons extra-virgin olive oil

Directions

Mix all the ingredients, except lemon juice and olive oil, in a large bowl.
Whisk together olive oil and lemon juice and pour over the salad; toss to combine well and serve.

Nutritional Information per Serving:

Calories: 180; Total Fat: 9 g; Carbs: 25 g; Dietary Fiber: 4 g; Sugars: 18 g; Protein: 3 g; Cholesterol: 0 mg; Sodium: 46 mg

23. Satisfying Turkey Lettuce Wraps

Yields: 4 Servings
Total Time: 35 Minutes
Prep Time: 15 Minutes
Cook Time: 20 Minutes

Ingredients

- 1/2 lb. ground turkey
- 1/2 small onion, finely chopped
- 1   garlic clove, minced
- 2   tablespoons extra virgin olive oil
- 1 head lettuce
- 1   teaspoon cumin
- 1/2 tablespoon fresh ginger, sliced
- 2   tablespoons apple cider vinegar
- 2 tablespoons freshly chopped cilantro
- 1 teaspoon freshly ground black pepper 1 teaspoon sea salt

Directions

Sauté garlic and onion in extra virgin olive oil until fragrant and translucent.

Add turkey and cook well.

Stir in the remaining ingredients and continue cooking for 5 minutes more.

To serve, ladle a spoonful of turkey mixture onto a lettuce leaf and wrap. Enjoy!

Nutrition Information per Serving:

Calories: 192; Total Fat: 13.6 g; Carbs: 4.6 g; Dietary Fiber: 1 g; Sugars: 1.2 g Protein: 16.3 g; Cholesterol: 58 mg; Sodium: 535 mg

24. Beautiful Berry Salad with Citrus-Strawberry Dressing

Yield: 3 Servings
Total Time: 5 Minutes
Prep Time: 5 Minutes
Cook Time: N/A

Ingredients

Salad

- ¼ cup blueberries
- ½ cup chopped strawberries
- 1 cup mixed greens (kale and chard)
- 2 cups baby spinach
- 2 chopped green onions
- ½ cup chopped avocado 1 shredded carrots

Dressing

- 1 tablespoon extra-virgin olive oil
- 2 tablespoons apple cider vinegar
- ¼ cup fresh orange juice 5 strawberries chopped

Directions

In a blender, blend together all dressing ingredients until very smooth; set aside.

Combine all salad ingredients in a large bowl; drizzle with dressing and toss to coat well before serving.

Nutritional Information per Serving:

Calories: 141; Total Fat: 7.4 g; Carbs: 17.4 g; Dietary Fiber: 5.5 g; Sugars: 7.5 g; Protein: 2.9 g; Cholesterol: 0 mg; Sodium: 42 mg

Yield: 3 Servings
Total Time: 20 Minutes
Prep Time: 5 Minutes
Cook Time: 15 Minutes

Ingredients

- 2 teaspoon sesame oil
- 1/2 cup diced carrots
- 1/2 cup chopped celery
- 1   cup chopped leeks or onions
- 2   garlic cloves, minced
- 1 teaspoon minced ginger
- 1   tablespoon date paste
- 2   tablespoons nut paste (walnuts and pumpkin seeds)
- 1-2 teaspoons lemon/lime juice
- 1   teaspoon allspice
- 1/4 teaspoon cardamom powder
- 2   teaspoons cumin powder
- A pinch of red chili flakes
- 1/2 teaspoon crushed black pepper
- Salt
- 4 cups vegetable broth
- 1/2 cup coarsely chopped spinach 1 cup
  cooked yellow mung beans

Directions

Heat oil in a stock pot over medium high heat; sauté chopped veggies and seasonings except spinach. Cook for about 10 minutes and then stir in, vegetable broth, spinach and mung beans; simmer for about 3 minutes and remove from heat.

Transfer the mixture to a food processor and blend until the soup is smooth. Serve the soup with small avocado cubes, garnished with tomatoes and parsley.

Nutritional Information per Serving:

Calories: 437; Total Fat: 38.7 g; Carbs: 19.6 g; Dietary Fiber: 8.9 g; Sugars: 5.2 g; Protein: 9.1 g; Cholesterol: 0 mg; Sodium: 153 mg

Yield: 2 Servings
Total Time: 10 Minutes + Chilling Time
Prep Time: 10 Minutes
Cook Time: N/A

Ingredients

- 1 cup shredded broccoli
- 1 cup shredded carrots
- 1/4 cup pineapple juice
- 1   tablespoon natural peanut butter
- 1/4 teaspoon red pepper flakes
- 3/4 teaspoon mild curry powder
- 2   tablespoons apple cider vinegar
- 4 drops liquid stevia
- 1/2 cup sliced grapes
- Handful roasted peanuts

Directions

In a serving bowl, combine broccoli and carrots.

In a small bowl, whisk together pineapple juice and peanut butter until smooth; whisk in red pepper flakes, curry powder and vinegar until well combined ; stir in stevia and pour over the broccoli slaw; toss to combine well and refrigerate for at least one hour or until flavors develop. Just before serving, stir in grapes and sprinkle with roasted peanuts. Enjoy!

Nutritional Information per Serving:

Calories: 126; Total Fat: 4.4 g; Carbs: 18.6 g; Dietary Fiber: 3.6 g; Sugars: 10.9 g; Protein: 4.6 g; Cholesterol: 0 mg; Sodium: 57 mg

Yield: 6 Servings
Total Time: Minutes
Prep Time: 10 Minutes
Cook Time: N/A

Ingredients

Wraps

- 4 large collard leaves, stems removed
- 1 medium avocado, sliced
- ½ cucumber, thinly sliced
- 1 cup diced mango
- 6 large strawberries, thinly sliced
- 6 (200g) grilled chicken breasts, diced 24 mint leaves

Dipping Sauce

- 2 tablespoons almond butter
- 2 tablespoons coconut cream
- 1   birds eye chili, finely chopped
- 2   tablespoons unsweetened applesauce
- ¼ cup fresh lime juice
- 1 teaspoon sesame oil
- 1 tablespoon apple cider vinegar
- 1 tablespoon tahini
- 1 clove garlic, crushed
- 1 tablespoon grated fresh ginger ⅛ teaspoon sea salt

Directions

For the wraps

Divide the veggies equally among the four large collard leaves; fold bottom edges over the filling, and then both sides and roll very tightly up to the end of the leaves; secure with toothpicks and cut each in half.

Make the sauce:

Combine all the sauce ingredients in a blender and blend until very smooth. Divide between bowls and serve with the wraps.

Nutritional Information per Serving:

Calories: 256; Total Fat: 15.8 g; Carbs: 20.2 g; Dietary Fiber: 6.6 g; Sugars: 10.1 g; Protein: 12.2 g; Cholesterol: 25 mg; Sodium: 43 mg

Yields: 3 Servings
Total Time: 35 Minutes
Prep Time: 10 Minutes
Cook Time: 25 Minutes

Ingredients

- 2 tablespoons extra virgin olive oil
- 14- ounce extra-firm tofu, sliced
- 1 medium onion, thinly sliced
- 1   medium yellow or red bell pepper, chopped
- 2   teaspoons grated fresh ginger
- 12 ounces spring greens, chopped 3 tablespoons teriyaki sauce
- 1/4 cup toasted cashews, chopped

Directions

Add half oil to a pan set over medium heat. Add tofu and fry until golden. Transfer to a plate.

Add the remaining oil to the pan and sauté onion until translucent. Stir in bell pepper and continue sautéing until onion is tender and golden. Stir in ginger and greens until wilted.

Stir in tofu and season with teriyaki sauce. Top with toasted cashews to serve.

Nutritional Information per Serving:

Calories: 338; Total Fat: 22.7 g; Carbs: 20.8 g; Dietary Fiber: 6.9 g; Protein: 19.3 g; Cholesterol: 0 mg; Sodium: 962 mg; sugars: 7.6 g

Yield: 2 Servings
29. Healthy Green Bean & Zucchini Sauté

Total Time: 15 Minutes
Prep Time: 5 Minutes
Cook Time: 10 Minutes

Ingredients

- 2 tablespoons extra virgin olive oil, divided
- 1/4cup green beans - cut into small pieces
- ½ small zucchini, thinly sliced
- A pinch of salt
- 2 tablespoons lemon juice
- 2 tablespoons sliced scallions

Directions

Add half of the oil to a skillet set over medium heat. Stir in green beans, zucchini, and salt and sauté, stirring, for about 9 minutes or until the veggies are crisp tender.

Remove the pan from heat and stir in lemon juice and scallions. Serve immediately.

Nutritional Information per Serving:

Yield: 3 Servings

Calories: 46; Total Fat: 3.7g; Carbs: 3.4g; Dietary Fiber: 1.4g; Protein: 1g; Cholesterol: 0mg; Sodium: 200mg; sugars: 1.1g

30. Master Cleanse Salad

Total Time: 10 Minutes
Prep Time: 10 Minutes
Cook Time: N/A

Ingredients

- 1 small red onion, sliced into thin rings
- 1 cup watercress, rinsed
- 1 zucchini, shaved
- 1 small broccoli head, rinsed and cut in small florets
- 1 avocado, diced
- 2 tablespoon s fresh lemon juice
- 1 tablespoon extra-virgin olive oil
- ½ teaspoon Dijon mustard
- ½ teaspoon sea salt
- ¼ cup crushed toasted almonds 1 tablespoon chia seeds

Directions

In a large bowl, mix together the veggies until well combined.

In a small bowl, whisk together lemon juice, olive oil, mustard and salt until well blended; pour over the salad and toss until well coated. Add almonds and chia seeds and toss to combine. Set the salad aside for at least 5 minutes for flavors to combine before serving.

Yield: 4 Servings
Nutritional Information per Serving:

Calories: 258; Total Fat: 22.1 g; Carbs: 14.1 g; Dietary Fiber: 7.7 g; Sugars: 3.5 g; Protein: 5.3 g; Cholesterol: 0 mg; Sodium: 352 mg

31. Raw Spicy Zoodle Bowl

Total Time: 10 Minutes
Prep Time: 10 Minutes Cook
Time: N/A

Ingredients

- 2 large carrots, spiralized
- 1 large zucchini, spiralized
- 1 cup fresh corn
- 1 cup purple cabbage, chopped
- 1 red bell pepper, thinly sliced
- 1/4 cup chopped fresh cilantro
- 1/2 cup chopped celery
- 3 tablespoons toasted sesame seeds

Spicy Dressing

Yield: 5 Servings

- ½ cup chopped green onions
- ½ cup chopped edamame
- ½ cup chopped cashews
- 1/2 tablespoon organic coconut oil
- ¼ cup fresh lime juice
- 1/2 cup diced avocado
- 1/4- inch piece of jalapeño
- 1-inch piece fresh ginger
- 1/4 - 1/3 cup of water
- 1 teaspoon liquid stevia
- 1/4 teaspoon sea salt A pinch of pepper

Directions

In a bender, blend together all the dressing ingredients until very smooth.

In a large bowl, combine carrots, zucchini, corn, purple cabbage, red pepper, cilantro, celery and sesame seeds; mix well. Pour the dressing over the salad mixture and toss to coat well. Enjoy!

Nutritional Information per Serving:

Calories: 317; Total Fat: 19.5 g; Carbs: 30.4 g; Dietary Fiber: 8.1 g; Sugars: 7.9 g; Protein: 11.7 g; Cholesterol: 0 mg; Sodium: 57 mg

32. Citrus Raw Kale Avocado Salad

Yield: 1 Serving

Total Time: 5 Minutes

Prep Time: 5 Minutes

Cook Time: N/A

Ingredients

- ½ ripe avocado, pitted, diced
- 1 bunch kale, stems removed and torn into bite-size pieces
- 1 tablespoon fresh lemon juice
- 1/8 teaspoon sea salt
- 1/8 teaspoon black pepper
- Toasted sesame seeds to garnish

Directions

In a large bowl, combine avocado and kale; using hands, massage the avocado into kale until kale is tender and well coated. Add lemon juice, salt and pepper and toss to coat well. Serve the salad garnished with sesame seeds.

Nutritional Information per Serving:

Calories: 242; Total Fat: 19.7 g; Carbs: 16.1 g; Dietary Fiber: 7.9 g; Sugars: 0.8 g; Protein: 4.1 g; Cholesterol: 0 mg; Sodium: 272 mg

33. Mixed Green & Salmon Salad with Toasted Walnuts

Yield: 6 Servings

Total Time: 25 Minutes

Prep Time: 15 Minutes

Cook Time: 10 Minutes

Ingredients

- 1 tablespoon extra-virgin olive oil
- 8 cup mixed greens (arugula, baby spinach, romaine lettuce)
- ¼ cup chopped toasted walnuts
- 2 teaspoons balsamic vinegar
- 1 teaspoon walnut oil ¼
- teaspoon sea salt
- ¾ pound salmon fillet
- Honey Mustard salad spray

Directions

In a skillet set over medium heat, toast walnuts for about 1 minute and transfer to a plate. Add half of the extra virgin olive oil to the same skillet and sauté half of the greens for about 1 minute; transfer to a salad bowl and repeat with the remaining oil and greens.

Add balsamic vinegar, walnut oil and salt to the salad and toss until well combined.

Place salmon in an ovenproof dish, skin side down and spray with salad spray; broil in a broiler on high for about 10 minutes or until cooked through. Remove the fish from the broiler and cut into 4 pieces; divide the green salad among four serving bowls and top each with one piece of fish. Enjoy!

Nutrition info Per Serving:

Calories: 238; Total Fat: 19.55 g; Carbs: 32.6 g; Dietary Fiber: 11.5 g; Sugars: 7.6 g; Protein: 20 g; Cholesterol: 25 mg; Sodium: 188 mg

Yield: 3 Servings

Total Time: 10 Minutes

Prep Time: 10 Minutes

Cook Time: N/A

Ingredients

Salad

- 1 cup chopped roasted chicken breast
- 1/2 avocado, chopped
- 1 cup baby spinach
- 1/3 red onion thinly sliced
- 1/2 cucumber, sliced
- 1 cup beans sprouts
- 1 carrot, grated
- 1 tomato, diced
- 1/2 cup fresh parsley
        8   almonds,   sliced

Dressing:

- 1   tablespoon extra virgin olive oil
- 2   tablespoons fresh lemon juice
- 1/74 teaspoon sea salt
- 1/4 teaspoon black pepper
- 1 teaspoon dried oregano

Directions

In a large bowl, mix all salad ingredients until well combined.

In a small bowl, whisk together all dressing ingredients until well blended and drizzle over the salad. Toss until well coated and serve.

Nutrition info Per Serving:

Calories: 229; Total Fat: 15.4 g; Carbs: 13.6 g; Dietary Fiber: 6 g; Sugars: 4.1 g; Protein: 11.9 g; Cholesterol: 25 mg; Sodium: 69 mg

Yield: 2 Servings

Total Time: 5 Minutes

Prep Time: 5 Minutes

Cook Time: N/A

Ingredients

Salad:

- 1/4 cup fresh blueberries
- 1/4 cup fresh pineapple chunks
- 2 cups Bibb lettuce
- 1/4 avocado, diced
- 1/3 cucumber, diced
- 1 tablespoon toasted almonds, chopped

Dressing

- 1/4 teaspoon chia seeds
- 1 tablespoon fresh lemon juice
- 1 tablespoon fresh orange juice
- 1 tablespoon extra-virgin olive oil
- 1/2 tablespoon raw honey

Directions

In a large bowl, mix all salad ingredients.

In a small bowl, whisk together all dressing ingredients until well blended; pour over the salad ingredients and toss to coat. Enjoy!

Nutrition info Per Serving:

Calories: 185; Total Fat: 13.7 g; Carbs: 16.9 g; Dietary Fiber: 3.4 g; Sugars: 10.6 g; Protein: 2.1 g; Cholesterol: 0 mg; Sodium: 8 mg

Yield: 4 Servings
Total Time: 25 Minutes
Prep Time: 10 Minutes Cook
Time: 15 Minutes

Ingredients:

- 2 tablespoons extra virgin olive oil
- 1 tablespoon minced garlic
- 1 large shallot, sliced
- 1 cup mushrooms, sliced
- 1 cup broccoli florets
- 1 cup artichoke hearts
- 1 bunch asparagus, sliced into 3-inch pieces
- 1 cup baby peas
- 1 cup cherry tomatoes, halved 1/2 teaspoon sea salt

Vinaigrette

- 3 tablespoons white wine vinegar
- 6 tablespoons extra-virgin olive oil
- 1/2 teaspoon sea salt 1 teaspoon
- ground oregano handful fresh
- parsley, chopped

Directions

Add oil to a skillet set over medium heat. Stir in garlic and shallots and sauté for about 2 minutes.

Stir in mushrooms for about 5 minutes or until golden. Stir in broccoli, artichokes, and asparagus and continue cooking for 5 more minutes. Stir in peas, tomatoes and salt and cook for 2 more minutes.

Prepare vinaigrette: mix together vinegar, oil, salt, oregano and parsley in a bowl until well combined.

Serve vegetable sauté in a serving bowl and drizzle with vinaigrette. Toss to combine and serve.

Nutritional Information per Serving:

Calories: 334; Total Fat: 28.6 g; Carbs: 18.3g; Dietary Fiber: 6.8g; Protein: 6.5g; Cholesterol: 0mg; Sodium: 530mg; sugars: 5.2g

37. Arugula, Avocado, & Orange Salad

Yield: 3 Servings
Total Time: 10 Minutes
Prep Time: 10 Minutes
Cook Time: N/A

Ingredients

- 2 mandarin oranges, peeled, cut sideways
- 1 avocado, peeled, thinly sliced
- Handful of arugula
- Handful of mint leaves
- Handful of basil
- ¼ cup pomegranate seeds
- ¼ cup shredded goat cheese

Vinaigrette:

- 1   tablespoon raw honey
- 2   tablespoons extra virgin olive oil
- 2 tablespoons fresh lemon juice
- 1/4 teaspoon sea salt
- ¼ teaspoon black pepper

Directions

In a large salad bowl, mix mandarin oranges, avocado, arugula, mint and basil until well combined.

In a small bowl, whisk together all vinaigrette ingredients until well blended. Pour over the salad and toss to coat well. Sprinkle the salad with pomegranate seeds and goat cheese and serve.

Nutrition info Per Serving:

Calories: 357; Total Fat: 29.5 g; Carbs: 18.5 g; Dietary Fiber: 7 g; Sugars: 8.5 g; Protein: 8.7 g; Cholesterol: 20 mg; Sodium: 239 mg

38. Healthy Cauliflower Cream Dill Soup

Yield: 3-4 Servings
Total Time: 40 Minutes
Prep Time: 10 Minutes
Cook Time: 30 Minutes

Ingredients

- 1   head chopped cauliflower
- 2   cups chicken broth
- 1 cup rice milk or soymilk
- 1 teaspoon dill
- A pinch of salt and pepper, to taste

Directions

Rinse cauliflower and chop.

Transfer the chopped cauliflower to a pot and add enough chicken broth to cover. Simmer over medium heat until tender. Blend the mixture, in batches, and return to the pot. Stir in milk to your desired consistency. Stir in dill and simmer for about 1 minute. Season with salt and pepper. Enjoy!

Nutritional Information per Serving:

Calories: 48; Total Fat: 0.6g; Carbs: 9.9g; Dietary Fiber: 1.7g; Protein: 1.5g; Cholesterol: 0mg; Sodium: 50mg; sugars: 1.6g

39. Fat-Burning Spinach & Beet Salad

Yield: 4 Servings
Total Time: 16 Minutes
Prep Time: 10 Minutes

Cook Time: 6 Minutes

Ingredients

- 1 tablespoon extra-virgin olive oil
- 1 cup thinly sliced red onion
- 1 clove garlic, minced
- 2 tablespoon chopped fresh parsley
- 2 tablespoon sliced Kalamata olives
- 2 plum tomatoes, chopped
- 2 tablespoons balsamic vinegar
- 2 cups beet wedges, steamed
- 1/4 teaspoon salt
- 8 cups baby spinach

Directions

Put spinach in a bowl.

Add oil to a skillet set over medium heat; add onion and sauté, stirring, for about 2 minutes or until tender. Stir in garlic, parsley, olives and tomatoes and cook, stirring for about 3 minutes or until tomatoes break down. Stir in vinegar, beets, and salt and continue cooking for 1 more minute or until the beets are heated through. Toss together spinach and beet mixture until well blended. Serve warm.

Nutritional Information per Serving:

Calories: 115; Total Fat: 4.5g; Carbs: 17.2g; Dietary Fiber: 4.5g; Protein: 4.4g; Cholesterol: 0mg; Sodium: 307mg; sugars: 10.8g

40. Citric Spinach Salad

Yield: 4 Servings
Total Time: 10 Minutes
Prep Time: 10 Minutes
Cook Time: N/A

Ingredients

- 1/2 small red onion, thinly sliced
- 2 tablespoons freshly squeezed orange or grapefruit juice
- 1 clove garlic, very finely chopped
- 1/2 teaspoon raw honey
- 1/2 tablespoon coarse-grain mustard
- 1 tablespoon extra-virgin olive oil
- 1 tablespoon white-wine vinegar
- 8 cups chopped spinach
- 1/4 teaspoon salt
- 1 teaspoon poppy seeds

Directions

Soak onion in a bowl of water for at least 10 minutes; drain and set aside.

In a salad bowl, combine orange (grapefruit) juice, garlic, honey, mustard, extra virgin olive oil, vinegar, and salt; stir in onion, spinach and fruit sections. Serve garnished with poppy seeds. **Nutritional Information per Serving:**

Calories: 287; Total Fat: 24.6g; Carbs: 14.4g; Dietary Fiber: 3.3g; Protein: 5.7g; Cholesterol: 0mg; Sodium: 154mg; sugars: 6.5g

41. Lean Steak with Oregano-Orange Chimichurri & Arugula Salad

Yield: 4 Servings
Total Time: 5 Minutes
Prep Time: 5 Minutes
Cook Time: 5 Minutes

Ingredients

- 1 teaspoon finely grated orange zest
- 1 teaspoon dried oregano
- 1 small garlic clove, grated
- 2 teaspoon vinegar (red wine, cider, or white wine)
- 1 tablespoon fresh orange juice
- 1/2 cup chopped fresh flat-leaf parsley leaves
- 1 1/2-pound lean steak, cut into 4 pieces
- Sea salt and pepper
- 1/4 cup and 2 teaspoons extra virgin olive oil
- 4 cups arugula
- 2 bulbs fennel, shaved
- 2 tablespoons whole-grain mustard

Directions

Make chimichurri: In a medium bowl, combine orange zest, oregano and garlic. Mix in vinegar, orange juice and parsley and then slowly whisk in ¼ cup of olive oil until emulsified. Season with sea salt and pepper.

Sprinkle the steak with salt and pepper; heat the remaining olive oil in a large skillet and cook steak over medium high heat for about 6 minutes per side or until browned. Remove from heat and let rest for at least 10 minutes.

Toss steak, greens, and fennel with mustard in a medium bowl; season with salt and pepper.

Serve steak with chimichurri and salad. Enjoy!

Nutritional Information per Serving:

Calories: 343; Total Fat: 20.6 g; Carbs: 2 g; Dietary Fiber: 0.5 g; Sugars: 0.8 g; Protein: 0.6 g; Cholesterol: 99 mg; Sodium: 146 mg

Yields: 2 Servings
Total Time: 30 Minutes
Prep Time: 15 Minutes
Cook Time: 15 Minutes

Ingredients

- 2 5-ounce portions of striped bass
- 2 tablespoons extra-virgin olive oil
- 1/2 lemon, juiced
- 1 fennel bulb, sliced
- 1/4 medium onion, sliced
- 1/4 cup chopped parsley
- 1 tablespoon capers, rinsed
- 1/2 teaspoon sea salt
- Chopped parsley and olive oil, for garnish

Directions

Add lemon juice, fennel and onion to a pan and cover with 1-inch water; bring the mixture to a gentle boil. Lower heat and simmer for about 5 minutes.

Add seasoned fish and sprinkle with parsley and capers; cover and simmer for about 10 minutes.

Transfer to a serving bowl and drizzle with extra virgin olive oil and top with more parsley to serve.

Nutritional Information per Serving:

Calories: 325; Total Fat: 24.6g; Carbs: 10.54g; Dietary Fiber: 4.3g; Protein: 10.9g; Cholesterol: 0mg; Sodium: 661mg; sugars: 0.7g

Yield: 1 Serving
Total Time: 5 Minutes
Prep Time: 5 Minutes
Cook Time: 5 Minutes

Ingredients

Salad:

- 1/2 cup chopped cooked chicken
- 1   cup shaved Brussels sprouts
- 2   cups baby spinach
- 2 cups mixed greens
- 1/2 avocado sliced
- Segments of one orange
- 1 teaspoon raw pumpkin seeds
- 1 teaspoon toasted almonds 1 teaspoon hemp seeds

Dressing:

- 1/2 shallot, chopped
- 1   garlic clove, chopped
- 2   teaspoons balsamic vinegar
- 1 teaspoon extra virgin olive oil
- ½ cup fresh orange juice
- 1 teaspoon Dijon mustard
- 1 teaspoon raw honey Fresh ground pepper

Directions

In a blender, blend together all dressing ingredients until very smooth; set aside.

Combine all salad ingredients in a large bowl; drizzle with dressing and toss to coat well before serving.

Nutritional Information per Serving:

Calories: 365; Total Fat: 15.6 g; Carbs: 39.8 g; Dietary Fiber: 12.5 g; Sugars: 14.2 g; Protein: 18.8 g; Cholesterol: 27 mg; Sodium: 142 mg

44. Pan-Seared Salmon Salad with Snow Peas & Grapefruit

Yield: 4 Servings
Total Time: 15 Minutes
Prep Time: 15 Minutes
Cook Time: N/A

Ingredients

- 4 (100g) skin-on salmon fillets
- 1/8 teaspoon sea salt
- 2 teaspoons extra virgin olive oil
- 4 cups arugula
- 8 leaves Boston lettuce, washed and dried
- 1   cup snow peas, cooked
- 2   avocados, diced

For Grapefruit-Dill Dressing:

- 1/4 cup grapefruit juice
- 1/4 cup extra virgin olive oil
- 1 teaspoon raw honey
- 1 tablespoon Dijon mustard
- 1   tablespoon chopped fresh dill
- 2   garlic cloves, minced1/2 teaspoon salt

Directions

Sprinkle fish with about 1/8 teaspoon salt and cook in 2 teaspoons of olive oil over medium heat for about 4 minutes per side or until golden.

In a small bowl, whisk together al dressing ingredients and set aside.

Divide arugula and lettuce among four serving plates

Divide lettuce and arugula among 4 plates and add the remaining salad ingredients; top each with seared salmon and drizzle with dressing. Enjoy!

Nutritional Information per Serving:

Calories: 608; Total Fat: 46 g; Carbs: 16.2 g; Dietary Fiber: 8.7 g; Sugars: 5.1 g; Protein: 38.9 g; Cholesterol: 78 mg; Sodium: 488 mg

Yield: 4 Servings
45. Stir-Fried Chicken with Water Chestnuts

Total Time: 25 Minutes
Prep Time: 10 Minutes
Cook Time: 15 Minutes

Ingredients

- 2 tablespoons sesame oil
- ¼ cup wheat-free tamari
- 4 small chicken breasts, sliced
- 1 small cabbage, chopped
- 3 garlic cloves, chopped
- 1 teaspoon Chinese five spice powder
- 1 cup dried plums
- 1 cup water chestnuts
Toasted sesame seeds

Directions

Heat sesame oil in a large skillet set over medium heat; stir in all the ingredients, except sesame seeds, and cook until cabbage and chicken are tender.

Serve warm sprinkled with toasted sesame seeds.

Yield: 4 Servings
Nutritional Information per Serving:

Calories: 306; Total Fat: 13.5 g; Carbs: 23.4 g; Dietary Fiber: 0.7 g; Sugars: 2 g; Protein: 22.5 g; Cholesterol: 62 mg; Sodium: 29 mg

46. Roasted Shrimp & Broccoli

Total Time: 20 Minutes
Prep Time: 10 Minute
Cook Time: 10 Minutes

Ingredients

- 5 cups broccoli florets
- 1 tablespoon fresh lemon juice
- 1 tablespoon grated lemon rind, divided
- 2 tablespoons extra-virgin olive oil
- Sea salt and pepper, divided 1 1/2
- pounds large shrimp
- 1/4 teaspoon crushed red pepper

Directions

Preheat oven to 425°.

Add broccoli to boiling water and cook for about 1 minute; transfer to iced water and drain.

In a bowl, combine lemon juice, 1 ½ teaspoons of lemon rind, olive oil, salt and pepper; add shrimp and toss to coat well. Arrange shrimp and

Yield: 4 Servings

broccoli on a greased pan and bake for about 8 minutes or until shrimp is cooked through.

In a large bowl, combine the remaining lemon rind, crushed red pepper, salt and pepper; toss in broccoli and serve with shrimp.

Nutritional Information per Serving:

Calories: 238; Total Fat: 7.4 g; Carbs: 11 g; Dietary Fiber: 3.1 g; Sugars: 2.1 g; Protein: 35.2 g; Cholesterol: 243 mg; Sodium: 251 mg

47. Sweet & Sour Chicken with Mixed Greens

Total Time: 40 Minutes
Prep Time: 10 Minutes
Cook Time: 30 Minutes

Ingredients

- ½ cup wheat-free tamari
- ½ cup apple cider vinegar
- ¼ cup brown rice syrup
- 1 large garlic cloves, minced
- 1 teaspoon ginger powder
- 2 chicken breasts, sliced
- 4 cups mixed greens
- 1 teaspoon toasted sesame seeds

Directions

Yield: 4 Servings

In a saucepan set over low heat, mix ginger, garlic, brown rice syrup, vinegar and tamari for about 12 minutes or until a thick sauce is formed. Add chicken pieces to the sauce and cook, stirring frequently, for about 15 minutes or until chicken is cooked through.

Pour the chicken sauce over mixed greens and sprinkle with toasted sesame seeds. Enjoy!

Nutritional Information per Serving:

Calories: 320; Total Fat: 5.8 g; Carbs: 40.2 g; Dietary Fiber: 8.2 g; Sugars: 18.3 g; Protein: 26.4 g; Cholesterol: 62 mg; Sodium: 258 mg

48. Steamed Salmon w/ Fennel & Fresh Herbs

Total Time: 21 Minutes
Prep Time: 15 Minutes
Cook Time: 6 Minutes

Ingredients

- 1 tablespoon extra-virgin olive oil
- 6 ounces wild salmon fillets, skinless
- Fennel fronds
- 1 tablespoon chopped parsley
- 1 tablespoon chopped dill
- 1 tablespoon chopped chives
- 1 tablespoon chopped tarragon
- 1 tablespoon chopped basil
-

Yield: 4 Servings
1 tablespoon chopped shallot 1
tablespoon lemon juice

Directions

Lightly oil a steamer basket with olive oil; add salmon and fennel wedges and steam for about 6 minutes. In a bowl, combine the chopped herbs, extra virgin olive oil, and shallot and lemon juice; stir until well combined. Season and spoon over cooked fish.

Nutritional Information per Serving:

Calories: 98; Total Fat: 6.3g; Carbs: 2.5g; Dietary Fiber: 0.9g; Protein: 8.9g; Cholesterol: 19mg; Sodium: 33mg; sugars: trace

Yield: 30 Servings
Total Time: 4 Hours 20 Minutes
Prep Time: 20 Minutes
Cook Time: 4 Hours

Ingredients

- 1   (8 to 10-pound) smoked ham, bone-in, skin on
- 2   cups tangerine juice
- 2 tangerines, sliced thin, seeds removed
- 1   cup (2 sticks) unsalted butter, cut in chunks
- 1/4 cup extra-virgin olive oil
- 2   teaspoons liquid stevia
- 1 1/2 pounds carrots, peeled
- 2 cinnamon sticks
- 1/4 tsp. whole cloves
- 1 cup water
- 1 bunch fresh sage

Sea salt & black pepper

Directions

Preheat oven to 300°F.

Place ham, fat-side down, in a roasting pan. Score the ham with ½-inch deep cuts across the skin, 2-inches apart with a sharp knife. Season with salt and pepper.

In a small bowl, mix oil and chopped sage leaves to make a paste; rub over the ham and bake for about 2 hours.

Meanwhile, make the glaze: set a large saucepan over medium heat; add tangerine juice, tangerines, butter, spices, stevia and water. Cook the mixture for about 40 minutes or until it forms a syrupy glaze.

After two hours of cooking ham, pour the tangerine glaze over it and scatter fruit pieces over it with the remaining sage leaves. Continue cooking for about 1 ½ hours more, basting with juices every 30 minutes.

Scatter the ham with carrots and continue cooking for 30 minutes more or until ham is dark and crispy and carrots are tender. Remove from oven and let cool before carving. Serve with tangerine and carrot glaze on side.

Nutrition info Per Serving:

Calories: 362; Total Fat: 20.8 g; Carbs: 17.2 g; Dietary Fiber: 4.3 g; Sugars: 7 g; Protein: 26 g; Cholesterol: 102 mg; Sodium: 2074 mg

50. Lemon Garlic Salmon

Yields: 4 Servings
Total Time: 35 Minutes
Prep Time: 15 Minutes
Cook Time: 30 Minutes

Ingredients

- 1 teaspoon extra virgin olive oil
- 4 salmon fillets
- 3 tablespoons freshly squeezed lemon juice
- 1 tablespoon coconut milk
- 1 teaspoon ground pepper
- 1 teaspoon dried parsley flakes 1
  finely chopped clove garlic

Directions

Preheat your oven to 190°C (275°F). Coat a baking dish with extra virgin olive oil.

Rinse the fish under water and pat dry with paper towels.

Arrange the fish fillet in the coated baking dish and drizzle with lemon juice and coconut oil. Sprinkle with ground pepper, parsley and garlic.

Bake in the oven for about 30 minutes or until the flakes easily when touched with a fork.

Nutritional Information per Serving:

Calories: 248; Total Fat: 12g; Carbs: 0.7g; Dietary Fiber: trace; Protein: 34.8g; Cholesterol: 0mg; Sodium: 82mg; trace

51. Perfect Grilled Pork Roast Served with Fruit Compote

Yield: 12 Servings
Total Time: 1 Hour 30 Minutes

Prep Time: 15 Minutes
Cook Time: 1 Hour 5 Minutes

Ingredients

- 1 (4-pound) pork loin roast, boneless, trimmed and tied with kitchen string
- 2 tablespoons extra virgin olive oil
- 2 tablespoons chopped garlic
- 2 teaspoons sea salt
- 1 teaspoon pepper
- 1 tablespoons chopped fresh thyme
- 1 tablespoons chopped fresh rosemary

Fruit Compote

- 1 apple, diced
- 1/2 cup red grapes, halved, seeds removed
- 12 dried apricots, sliced
- 16 dried figs, coarsely chopped
- 1/2 cup chopped red onion
- 1/2 cup cider vinegar
- 1/2 cup dry white wine
- 2 teaspoons liquid stevia
- 1/2 teaspoon salt
- 1/2 teaspoon pepper

Directions

In a small bowl, stir together thyme, rosemary, garlic, salt and pepper and rub the mixture over the pork.

Light one side of your grill and heat to 400°F, leaving the other side unlit; place the pork on the lit side and cover; grill for about 10 minutes per side or until browned. Transfer the pork to the unlit side and cover; grill for about 45 minutes or until internal temperature reads 150°F. Remove from heat and let stand for about 10 minutes before slicing. Serve pork with fruit compote.

Make Fruit Compote:

In a saucepan, combine all ingredients and cook over medium heat, stirring, for about 25 minutes or until liquid is reduced to a quarter.

Nutrition info Per Serving:

Calories: 442; Total Fat: 17.5 g; Carbs: 24.4 g; Dietary Fiber: 4 g; Sugars: 17.6 g; Protein: 44.8 g; Cholesterol: 122 mg; Sodium: 577 mg

52. Mango Chili Chicken Stir Fry

Yield: 4 Servings
Total Time: 30 Minutes
Prep Time: 25 Minutes
Cook Time: 5 Minutes

Ingredients

- ½ tablespoon sesame oil
- 1 tablespoon low-sodium soy sauce
- 1 tablespoon cornstarch
- 1 pound chicken thighs, skinless, boneless, diced
- ½ tablespoon peanut oil
- 1 tablespoon minced fresh ginger
- 1   red onion, chopped
- 2   cups snow peas
- 1 tablespoon chili garlic sauce
- 1 mango, peeled, chopped
- 1/8 teaspoon sea salt

1/8 teaspoon black pepper

Directions

In a large mixing bowl, combine sesame oil, soy sauce, cornstarch and chicken; let sit for at least 20 minutes.

In a large skillet, heat peanut oil and then sauté ginger and onion for about 2 minutes; add snow peas and stir fry for about 1 minute. Add chicken with the marinade and stir fry for about 2 minutes or until chicken is browned. Add chili sauce, mango and pepper and continue stir frying for 1 minute or until chicken is cooked through and mango is tender. Serve the stir fry over cooked brown rice.

Nutrition info Per Serving:

Calories: 354; Total Fat: 12.4 g; Carbs: 23.8 g; Dietary Fiber: 4.3 g; Sugars: 16.2 g; Protein: 36.8 g; Cholesterol: 101 mg; Sodium: 382 mg

53. Tasty Sesame Salmon

Yield: 3 Servings
Total Time: 30 Minutes + Chilling Time
Prep Time: 5 Minutes
Cook Time: 25 Minutes

Ingredients

- 1 teaspoon dried chili flakes
- 1   teaspoon minced ginger root
- 2   tablespoon rice vinegar
- 2 tablespoons soy sauce
- 1 large clove garlic, minced
- 3 skinless wild salmon fillets
- 3 tablespoons white sesame seeds

Directions

In a zip-top bag, mix chili flakes, ginger, rice vinegar, soy sauce, and garlic; add salmon filets in the bag and refrigerate for at least 1 hour.

Preheat oven to 375°F.

Sprinkle sesame seeds onto a plate into a single layer; arrange the filets, face down, in the sesame seeds and transfer the fish onto a baking sheet lined with baking paper; sprinkle with more sesame seeds and bake for about 20 minutes. Switch the oven to broil the fish for about 5 minutes or until sesame seeds are toasted.

Nutrition info Per Serving:

Calories: 248; Total Fat: 11 g; Carbs: 0.9 g; Dietary Fiber: 4 g; Sugars: 17.6 g; Protein: 35.2 g; Cholesterol: 78 mg; Sodium: 680 mg

54. Veggie & Beef Salad Bowl

Yield: 2 Servings
Total Time: 25 Minutes

Prep Time: 10 Minutes
Cook Time: 15 Minutes

Ingredients

- 2   tablespoons dry red quinoa
- 1/2 cup chopped broccoli florets
- 3   ounces cooked lean beef, diced
- 2 cups mixed greens (arugula, baby spinach, romaine lettuce)
- 1/4 red bell pepper, chopped
- 1   teaspoon red wine vinegar
- 2   teaspoons extra virgin olive oil

Directions

Follow package directions to cook quinoa.

In a large bowl, toss cooked quinoa with broccoli, beef, greens, and bell pepper.

In a small bowl, whisk together vinegar and oil and pour over the salad. Serve.

Nutrition info Per Serving:

Calories: 145; Total Fat: 4.2 g; Carbs: 16.6 g; Dietary Fiber: 4.8 g; Sugars: 3.4 g; Protein: 10.2 g; Cholesterol: 19 mg; Sodium: 50 mg

55. Baked Salmon with Dill-Avocado Yogurt

Yield: 4 Servings
Total Time: 20 Minutes
Prep Time: 10 Minutes
Cook Time: 10 Minutes

Ingredients

- 1/2 cup Greek yogurt
- 1 avocado, diced
- 2 tablespoons lemon juice
- 1 clove garlic
- 3 tablespoons chopped dill
- 4 (6-ounce) salmon fillets
- 1 tablespoon extra-virgin olive oil
- Pinch of sea salt
- Pinch of black pepper

Directions

Preheat oven to 400°F.

In a blender, blend together Greek yogurt, avocado, 1 tablespoon water, lemon juice, garlic, dill, salt and pepper until very smooth; set aside.

Place salmon skin side down onto a foil lined baking sheet and drizzle with extra virgin olive oil; season with salt and pepper and bake for about 10 minutes or until cooked through. Serve salmon topped with dill-avocado yogurt.

Nutrition info Per Serving:

Calories: 388; Total Fat: 24.5 g; Carbs: 7.2 g; Dietary Fiber: 3.7 g; Sugars: 1.6 g; Protein: 37.4 g; Cholesterol: 76 mg; Sodium: 52 mg

56. Crock Pot Coconut Curry Shrimp

Yield: 8 Servings
Total Time: 2 Hours 5 Minutes
Prep Time: 5 Minutes
Cook Time: 2 Hours

Ingredients

- 1 pound shrimp, with shells
- 15 ounces water
- 30 ounces light coconut milk
- ½ cup Thai red curry sauce
- ¼ cup cilantro
- 2½ teaspoon lemon garlic seasoning

Directions

In a slow cooker, combine water, coconut milk, red curry paste, cilantro, and lemon garlic seasoning; stir to mix well and cook on high for about 2 hours. Add shrimp and continue cooking for another 30 minutes or until shrimp is cooked through.

Serve garnished with cilantro.

Nutrition info Per Serving:

Calories: 312; Total Fat: 26.3 g; Carbs: 6.8 g; Dietary Fiber: 2.3 g; Sugars: 3.5 g; Protein: 15.3 g; Cholesterol: 119 mg; Sodium: 156 mg

57. Delicious Baked Tilapia in Garlic & Olive Oil

Yields: 4 Servings
Total Time: 35 Minutes
Prep Time: 15 Minutes
Cook Time: 30 Minutes

Ingredients

- 4 (4 ounce) tilapia fillets
- 4 cloves crushed garlic
- 3 tablespoons extra-virgin olive oil
- 1 chopped onion
- 1/4 teaspoon salt

Directions

Rub the tilapia fillets with garlic and arrange them in a baking dish. Drizzle the fish with olive oil until well coated and top with onion. Refrigerate the fish, covered, for at least 8 hours or overnight to soak in the marinade.

When ready, preheat your oven to 175°C (350°F).

Transfer the fish fillets to a 9x13 inch baking dish; pour over the marinade mixture and sprinkle with salt. Bake the fish for about 30 minutes.

Nutritional Information per Serving:

Calories: 194; Total Fat: 11.6g; Carbs: 2.6g; Dietary Fiber: 0.6g; Protein: 21.4g; Cholesterol: 0mg; Sodium: 154mg; sugars: 1.2g

58. Turkey w/ Capers, Tomatoes, and Greens Beans

Yield: 4 Servings
Total Time: 35 Minutes
Prep Time: 15 Minutes
Cook Time: 20 Minutes

Ingredients

- 1 tablespoon extra-virgin olive oil
- 6 ounces turkey
- ¼ cup capers
- ¼ cup diced fresh tomatoes
- Steamed green beans for serving

Directions

Heat oil in a pan; add turkey and fry until golden brown and cooked through.

Remove the cooked turkey from the pan and transfer to a plate; add capers and tomatoes to the pan and cook until juicy. Spoon the caper mixture over the turkey and serve with steamed green beans.

Nutritional Information per Serving:

Calories: 111; Total Fat: 5.7g; Carbs: 1.8g; Dietary Fiber: 0.9g; Protein: 5.7g; Cholesterol: 32mg; Sodium: 286mg; sugars: 0.5g

59. Grilled Tuna w/ Bean & Tomato Salad

Yields: 4 Servings
Total Time: 19 Minutes
Prep Time: 15 Minutes
Cook Time: 4 Minutes

Ingredients

- 1 1/2 tablespoons extra-virgin olive oil
- 3 scallions, thinly sliced
- 1 tablespoon fresh lemon juice
- 1/4 cup fresh tarragon leaves
- 1 (15 ounces) can beans, drained, rinsed
- 1 pound heirloom tomatoes , cored, diced
- Sea salt
- 4 (8 ounce) tuna steaks

Directions

In a bowl, mix together oil, scallions, lemon juice, tarragon, beans, tomatoes, and salt; set aside.

Lightly grease the grill grates with oil and heat to medium. Season tuna with salt and grill for about 4 minutes or until cooked through. Serve tuna with bean salad.

Nutritional Information per Serving:

Calories: 505; Total Fat: 19.8g; Carbs: 9.4g; Dietary Fiber: 4g; Protein: 70.4g; Cholesterol: 111mg; Sodium: 123mg; sugars: 1.8g

60. Teriyaki Fish w/ Zucchini

Yields: 2 Servings
Total Time: 20 Minutes
Prep Time: 10 Minutes
Cook Time: 10 Minutes

Ingredients

- 2 (6-ounce) salmon fillets
- 7 tablespoons teriyaki sauce (low-sodium)
- 2 tablespoons sesame seeds
- 2 teaspoons canola oil
- 4 scallions, chopped
- 2 small zucchini, thinly sliced

Directions

Mix fish with 5 tablespoons of teriyaki sauce in a zip-top bag and marinate for at least 20 minutes.

In a skillet set over medium heat, toast sesame seeds; set aside. Drain the marinated fish and discard the marinade.

Add fish to the skillet and cook for about 5 minutes; remove fish from skillet and keep warm.

Add oil, scallions and zucchini to the skillet and sauté for about 4 minutes or until browned.

Stir in the remaining teriyaki sauce and sprinkle with toasted sesame seeds; serve with fish.

Nutritional Information per Serving:

Calories: 408; Total Fat: 19.9 g; Carbs: 18.1 g; Dietary Fiber: 4.3 g; Protein: 40.3 g; Cholesterol: 75 mg; Sodium: 2505 mg; sugars: 11.7 g

HEALTHY INTERMITTENT SNACKS/DESSERTS

61. Grain-Free Mixed Seed Crackers

Yield: 5 Servings
Total Time: 1 Hour 10 Minutes
Prep Time: 10 Minutes
Cook Time: 1 Hour

Ingredients

- 1/4 cup amaranth 1/4 cup
- flaxseeds
- 1   tablespoon sesame seeds
- 2   tablespoons black chia seeds
- 1/2 cup sunflower seeds
- 1/4 cup pepitas
- 3/4 cup warm water 1
- teaspoon sea salt

Directions

In a bowl, mix together amaranth, seeds, and pepitas; add in warm water and let sit until all water in absorbed. Stir in salt and pepper.

Meanwhile, preheat your oven to 320 degrees and line a baking tray with paper.

Spread the amaranth mixture onto the tray and bake in the oven for about 1 hour or until golden and crispy. Cut into 20 bars and serve.

Nutrition information per Serving:

Calories: 255; Total Fat: 4.4 g; Carbs: 2.6 g; Dietary Fiber: 2 g; Sugars: 0.2 g; Protein: 2.5 g; Cholesterol: 0 mg; Sodium: 107 mg

62. Citrus Avocado Snack

Yield: 4 Servings
Total Time: 10 Minutes

Prep Time: 10 Minutes
Cook Time: N/A

Ingredients

- 2 avocados, diced
- 1   seedless orange, cut into segments
- 2   small red onions, minced
- 2 teaspoons apple cider vinegar
- 2 cups shredded lettuce
- 2 plum tomatoes, sliced Salt and
  pepper

Directions

Combine the avocado, lettuce, orange segments, onion, vinegar, cilantro, salt and pepper; toss well to combine and serve right away.

Nutritional Info Per Serving:

Calories: 259; Fat: 19.9g; Carbs: 21.3 g; Dietary Fiber: 9.4 g; Sugars: 9 g; Protein: 3.6 g; Cholesterol: 0 mg; Sodium: 17 mg

63. Apricots & Walnuts Snack

Yield: 1 Serving
Total Time: 5 Minutes
Prep Time: 5 Minutes
Cook Time: N/A

Ingredients

- 7   walnut   halves   5
- dried apricots

Directions

In a small bowl, combine the walnuts and apricots. Enjoy!

Nutrition information per Serving:

Calories:134; Total Fat: 9 g; Carbs: 13 g; Dietary Fiber: 2 g; Sugars: 10 g; Protein: 3 g; Cholesterol: 0 mg; Sodium: 2 mg

64. Anti-Inflammatory Trail Mix

Yield: 5 Servings
Total Time: 5 Minutes
Prep Time: 5 Minutes
Cook Time: N/A

Ingredients

- ¼ cup unsalted roasted peanuts
- ¼ cup whole shelled almonds
- ¼ cup chopped pitted dates
- ¼ cup dried cranberries 2
- ounces dried apricots

Directions

In a medium bowl, mix together all the ingredients until well combined. Enjoy!

Nutrition information per Serving:

Calories: 132; Total Fat: 7 g; Carbs: 15 g; Dietary Fiber: 3 g; Sugars:

10 g; Protein: 4 g; Cholesterol: 0 mg; Sodium: 0 mg

65. Crispy Lemon- Chili Roasted Kale

Yield: 2 Servings
Total Time: 30 Minutes
Prep Time: 10 Minutes
Cook Time: 20 Minutes

Ingredients

- 2 bunches kale, ribs and stems removed, roughly chopped
- 2 tablespoons lemon juice
- 2 tablespoons extra-virgin olive oil
- 1   teaspoon lemon salt
- 2   teaspoons chili powderParmesan wedge

Directions

Preheat oven to 250°F.

In a large bowl, massage together kale, lemon juice, extra virgin olive oil, lemon salt and chili powder until kale is tender; spread the kale on a baking sheet and bake for about 20 minutes or until crisp tender. Remove from oven and sprinkle with parmesan cheese. Serve warm.

Nutrition info Per Serving:

Calories: 165; Total Fat: 14.6 g; Carbs: 8.7 g; Dietary Fiber: 2 g; Sugars: 0.5 g; Protein: 2.4 g; Cholesterol: 0 mg; Sodium: 58 mg

66. Citrus Greek Yogurt

Yield: 4 Servings
Total Time: 13 Minutes
Prep Time: 10 Minutes
Cook Time: 3 Minutes

Ingredients

- 3 cups nonfat Greek yogurt
- 1 tablespoon orange zest
- 1/4 cup good honey
- 1 1/2 teaspoons pure vanilla extract
- 1/4 cup chopped roasted walnuts, plus more to garnish
- 1/4 cup raisins
- ½ cup freshly orange juice ½ cup fresh lemon juice

Directions

In a large bowl, combine Greek yogurt, orange zest, honey, vanilla, walnuts and raisins and stir to mix well. Whisk in lemon and orange juice and refrigerate until chilled. Serve chilled garnished with more roasted walnuts. Enjoy!

Nutrition info Per Serving:

Calories: 296; Total Fat: 8.4 g; Carbs: 36.5 g; Dietary Fiber: 1.2 g; Sugars: 33.1; Protein: 19.8 g; Cholesterol: 9 mg; Sodium: 64 mg

67. Curried Cashews

Yield: 8 Servings
Total Time: 16 Minutes
Prep Time: 5 Minutes
Cook Time: 11 Minutes

Ingredients

- 2 cups roasted cashews
- 2 tablespoons salted butter
- 1/4 teaspoon cayenne
- 4 teaspoons curry powder 1
- teaspoon sea salt

Directions

Preheat oven to 350°F.

In a small skillet set over medium heat, melt butter and then add cayenne pepper, curry powder and salt; cook for about 30 seconds or until fragrant.

In a baking sheet, toss together the curry butter and cashews until well coated and then spread the cashews in a single layer. Bake for about 10 minutes or until hot and shiny. Cool to room temperature before serving.

Nutrition info Per Serving:

Calories: 225; Total Fat: 18.9 g; Carbs: 11.8 g; Dietary Fiber: 1.4 g; Sugars: 1.8; Protein: 5.4 g; Cholesterol: 8 mg; Sodium: 260 mg

68. Spicy Yogurt Dip with Veggies

Yield: 8 Servings
Total Time: 10 Minutes
Prep Time: 10 Minutes
Cook Time: N/A

Ingredients

- 4 cups nonfat Greek yogurt
- 1 teaspoon onion powder 1
- teaspoon garlic powder
- 1 teaspoon sea salt
- ¼ cup chopped parsley
-

Cut-up fresh veggies (cucumbers, carrots, celery sticks, bell peppers)

Directions

In a bowl, combine yogurt, onion powder, garlic powder, and salt; whisk to mix well. Stir in chopped parsley and serve the dip with fresh veggies.

Nutrition info Per Serving:

Calories: 34; Total Fat: 0 g; Carbs: 5 g; Dietary Fiber: 1 g; Sugars: 43.6; Protein: 4 g; Cholesterol: 0 mg; Sodium: 85 mg

69. Bell Pepper Candies

Yield: 6 Servings
Total Time: 8 Hours 5 Minutes
Prep Time: 5 Minutes
Cook Time: 8 Hours

Ingredients

- 2 red bell peppers, seeds removed, and sliced into ½-inch pieces 1
- tablespoon maple syrup

Directions

Drizzle the bell peppers with maple syrup and toss until well coated. Preheat oven to 150°F.

Place wire rack over a cookie sheet and cover with parchment paper. Arrange the bell peppers over the parchment paper and place in the center of oven rack. Let the bell peppers dehydrate for about 8 hours or until crispy.

Nutrition info Per Serving:

Calories: 21; Total Fat: 0.1 g; Carbs: 5.2 g; Dietary Fiber: 0.5 g; Sugars: 4; Protein: 0.4 g; Cholesterol: 0 mg; Sodium: 1 mg

70. Veggies with Almond-Butter Dip

Yield: 1 Serving

Total Time: 5 Minutes

Prep Time: 5 Minutes

Cook Time: N/A

Ingredients

- 1 teaspoon apple cider vinegar
- 1 tablespoon fresh orange juice
- 4 teaspoons almond butter
- 2 teaspoons peanuts
- 2 cups sliced cucumber, 1 cup sliced baby carrots or 1 cup sliced bell peppers

Directions

In a bowl, whisk vinegar, orange juice and almond butter until smooth. Top with peanuts.
Serve the veggies with the dip for dipping.

Nutritional Information per Serving:

Calories: 200; Total Fat: 14 g; Carbs: 15 g; Dietary Fiber: 3 g; Sugars: 3.7 g; Protein: 3.1 g; Cholesterol: 0 mg; Sodium: 105 mg

71. Warm Lemon Rosemary Olives

Yields: 12 Servings
Total Time: 35 Minutes
Prep Time: 5 Minutes
Cook Time: 20 Minutes

Ingredients

- 1 teaspoon extra-virgin olive oil
- 1 teaspoon grated lemon peel
- 1 teaspoon crushed red pepper flakes
- 2 sprigs fresh rosemary
- 3 cups mixed olives
- Lemon twists, optional

Directions

Preheat your oven to 400°F. Place pepper flakes, rosemary, olives and grated lemon peel onto a large sheet of foil; drizzle with oil and fold the foil. Pinch the edges of the sheet to tightly seal.

Bake in the preheated oven for about 30 minutes. Remove from the sheet and place the mixture to serving dish. Serve warm garnished with lemon twists.

Nutritional Information per Serving:

Calories: 43; Total Fat: 4 g; Carbs: 2.2 g; Dietary Fiber: 1.1 g; Protein: 0.3 g; Cholesterol: 0 mg; Sodium: 293 mg; Sugars: trace

72. Creamy Cucumbers

Yield: 2 Servings
Total Time: 15 Minutes
Prep Time: 15 minutes
Cook Time: 0 Minutes

Ingredients

- 2 English cucumbers, thinly sliced
- 1   ½ cups low fat Greek yoghurt
- 2   tablespoons lemon juice, fresh
- 1 ½ teaspoons mustard seeds
- Coarse salt and ground pepper, to taste
- Small bunch dill

Directions

Combine all the ingredients in a bowl until well combined.

Nutritional Information per Serving:

Calories: 250; Total Fat: 5.6 g; Carbs: 32.4 g; Dietary Fiber: 5.2 g; Protein: 24.6 g; Cholesterol: 8 mg; Sodium: 114 mg; Sugars: 12.4 g

73. Vinegar & Salt Kale Chips

Yield: 2 Servings
Total Time: 22 Minutes
Prep Time: 10 Minutes
Cook Time: 12 Minutes

Ingredients

- 1 head kale, chopped
- 1 teaspoon extra virgin olive oil
- 1 tablespoon apple cider vinegar ½
- teaspoon sea salt

Directions

Place kale in a bowl and drizzle with vinegar and extra virgin olive oil; sprinkle with salt and massage the ingredients with hands.

Spread the kale out onto two paper-lined baking sheets and bake at 375°F for about 12 minutes or until crispy.

Let cool for about 10 minutes before serving.

Nutritional Information per Serving:

Calories: 152; Total Fat: 8.2 g; Carbs: 15.2 g; Dietary Fiber: 2 g; Protein: 4 g; Cholesterol: 0 mg; Sodium: 1066 mg; Sugars: trace

74. Healthy Stuffed Mushrooms

Yield: 4 Servings
Total Time: 20 Minutes
Prep Time: 10 Minutes
Cook Time: 10 Minutes

Ingredients

- 1 cup parsley, chopped
- 1 teaspoon lemon juice
- 1 clove garlic, chopped ½ cup
- pine nuts
- ½ cup sun dried tomatoes
- ¼ teaspoon sea salt
- ¼ cup extra virgin olive oil
- 1 package (8 ounce) mushrooms

Directions

Pulse parsley in a food processor until well chopped.

Add lemon juice, garlic, pine nuts, sundried tomatoes and salt and continue pulsing until smooth.

Add extra virgin olive oil and pulse to blend well.

Remove the stems from mushrooms; stuff each with pesto and bake at 350°F for about 10 minutes.

Nutritional Information per Serving:

Calories: 271; Total Fat: 26.5 g; Carbs: 8.5 g; Dietary Fiber: 2.5 g; Protein: 5.3 g; Cholesterol: 0 mg; Sodium: 166 mg; Sugars: 1.8 g

75. Squash Fries

Yield: 1 Servings
Total Time: 20 Minutes
Prep Time: 10 Minutes
Cook Time: 10 Minutes

Ingredients

- 1 medium butternut squash
- 1 teaspoon extra-virgin olive oil
- 1 tablespoon grapeseed oil 1/8
- teaspoon sea salt

Directions

Peel and remove seeds from the squash; cut into thin slices and place them in a bowl. Coat with extra virgin olive oil and grapeseed oil; sprinkle with salt and toss to coat well.

Arrange the squash slices onto three baking sheets and broil in the oven until crispy.

Nutritional Information per Serving:

Calories: 192; Total Fat: 12.9 g; Carbs: 18.2 g; Dietary Fiber: 2.5 g; Protein: 1.7 g; Cholesterol: 0 mg; Sodium: 220 mg; Sugars: 3.5 g

76. Delicious Ginger Tahini Dip

Yield: 8 Servings
Total Time: 5 Minutes
Prep Time: 5 Minutes
Cook Time: N/A

Ingredients

- ½ cup tahini

- 1   teaspoon grated garlic
- 2   teaspoons ground turmeric
- 1 tablespoon grated fresh ginger
- ¼ cup apple cider vinegar
- ¼ cup water
- ½ teaspoon salt

Directions

In a bowl, whisk together tahini, turmeric, ginger, water, vinegar, garlic, and salt until well blended. Serve with assorted veggies.

Nutrition information per Serving:

Calories: 92; Total Fat: 8 g; Carbs: 4 g; Dietary Fiber: 1 g; Sugars: 0 g; Protein: 3 g; Cholesterol: 0 mg; Sodium: 151 mg;

77. Carrot French Fries

Yield: 2 Servings
Total Time: 35 Minutes
Prep Time: 15 Minutes
Cook Time: 20 Minutes

Ingredients

- 6 large carrots
- 2 tablespoons extra virgin olive oil ½
- teaspoon sea salt

Directions

Chop the carrots into 2-inch sections and then cut each section into thin sticks.

Toss together the carrots sticks with extra virgin olive oil and salt in a bowl and spread into a baking sheet lined with parchment paper.

Bake the carrot sticks at 425° for about 20 minutes or until browned.

Nutritional Information per Serving:

Calories: 209; Total Fat: 14 g; Carbs: 21.2 g; Dietary Fiber: 5.3 g; Protein: 1.8 g; Cholesterol: 0 mg; Sodium: 617 mg; Sugars: 10.6 g

78. Candied Macadamia Nuts

Yield: 2 Servings
Total Time: 25 Minutes
Prep Time: 10 Minutes
Cook Time: 15 Minutes

Ingredients

- 2 cups macadamia nuts
- 1   tablespoon extra-virgin olive oil
- 2   tablespoons agave nectar or honey½ teaspoon sea
- salt

Directions

In a bowl, toss together all ingredients and spread into a baking dish. Bake at 350°F for about 15 minutes or until browned. Remove
from oven and let cool before serving.

Nutritional Information per Serving:

Calories: 602; Total Fat: 58.9 g; Carbs: 23.3 g; Dietary Fiber: 5.9 g; Protein: 5.7 g; Cholesterol: 0 mg; Sodium: 436 mg; Sugars: 20.1 g

79. Healthy Pistachio & Dark Chocolate Kiwi

Yield: 1 Serving
Total Time: 5 Minutes
Prep Time: 5 Minutes
Cook Time: N/A

Ingredients

- 2 teaspoons melted dark chocolate
- 1   kiwi, sliced
- 2   tablespoons salted roasted chopped pistachios

Directions

Place kiwi in a bowl and drizzle with melted chocolate. Sprinkle with pistachios and serve right away.

Nutrition information per Serving:

Calories: 142; Total Fat: 7 g; Carbs: 20 g; Dietary Fiber: 3 g; Sugars: 13 g; Protein: 2 g; Cholesterol: 1 mg; Sodium: 22 mg

80. Spicy Peanut Masala

Yield: 8 Servings
Total Time: 10 Minutes
Prep Time: 10 Minutes
Cook Time: N/A

Ingredients

- 2 cup peanuts roasted
- 1   teaspoon red chili powder
- 2   tablespoons cilantro
- 1 teaspoon lemon juice 1
- teaspoon chai masala
- 1/2 cup chopped tomato
- 1/2 cup chopped onion 1
- teaspoon salt

Directions

Mix all ingredients in a large bowl until well combined. Serve.

Nutritional Information per Serving:

Calories: 420; Total Fat: 35.2 g; Carbs: 16.5 g; Dietary Fiber: 6.1 g; Sugars: 3.6 g; Protein: 17 g; Cholesterol: 0 mg; Sodium: 871 mg

HEALTHY INTERMITTENT DRINKS

81. Chilled Ginger Lemon Pomegranate Juice

Yield: 1 Serving
Total Time: 10 Minutes
Prep Time: 10 Minutes
Cook Time: N/A

Ingredients

- 1 cup pomegranate seeds
- 1 cup freshly squeezed lemon juice
- ¼ cup apple cider vinegar
- 1 large knob fresh ginger root

Directions

Combine everything in a blender and blend until smooth; strain out the juice through a fine mesh and serve chilled.

Nutritional Information per Serving:

Calories: 178; Total Fat: 2.1 g; Carbs: 21.8 g; Dietary Fiber: 2.1 g; Sugars: 17.6 g; Protein: 3.1 g; Cholesterol: 0 mg; Sodium: 52 mg

82. Chilled Metabolism Detox Drink

Yield: 1 Serving
Total Time: 5 Minutes + Chilling Time
Prep Time: 5 Minutes
Cook Time: N/A

Ingredients

- 4 cups filtered water
- 2 tablespoons minced fresh ginger
- 1/2 cup freshly squeezed lemon juice
- 1 teaspoon apple cider vinegar
- 1/4 teaspoon cayenne pepper 1
- teaspoon cinnamon

Directions

Mince ginger and stir in water; squeeze out the liquid and add to a mixing jug; stir in cinnamon powder, fresh lemon juice, apple cider vinegar, and cayenne pepper.

Refrigerate until chilled. Enjoy!

Nutritional Information per Serving:

Calories: 22; Total Fat: 0.1 g; Carbs: 6 g; Dietary Fiber: 1 g; Sugar: 1 g; Protein: 0.5 g; Cholesterol: 0 mg; Sodium: 9 mg

83. Delicious Strawberry Punch

Serving Total: 9 servings
Total Time: 5 Minutes
Prep Time: 5 Minutes Cook
Time: N/A

Ingredients:

- 1 cup fresh strawberries
- 4 cups diet ginger ale
- 4 cups fresh pineapple juice

Directions:

Blend the strawberries until smooth. Add ginger ale and pineapple juice and chill for at least 24 hours. Garnish with lime or lemon wedges, if desired.

Nutritional Information per Serving:

Calories: 63; Total Fat: 0.1 g; Carbs: 16 g; Dietary Fiber: trace; Protein: 0.6 g; Cholesterol: 0 mg; Sodium: 8 mg; sugars: 12.1 g

84. Lime Dried Hibiscus Tea

Yield: 1 Serving
Total Time: 10 Minutes
Prep Time: 10 Minutes
Cook Time: N/A

Ingredients

- 1 cup dried hibiscus flower
- 1 cup water
- 1 cup freshly squeezed lime juice 1
- teaspoon raw honey

Directions

Combine hibiscus flower and cold water and steep overnight in the fridge or until the color is faded from the flowers. Strain the liquid through a fine mesh and into a serving cup; stir in fresh lime juice and raw honey and serve.

Nutritional Information per Serving:

Calories: 32; Total Fat: 0 g; Carbs: 9.5 g; Dietary Fiber: 0.2 g; Sugars: 6.5 g; Protein: 0.2 g; Cholesterol: 0 mg; Sodium: 8 mg

85. Citrus Punch

Serving Total: 2 servings
Total Time: 5 Minutes

Prep Time: 5 Minutes Cook
Time: N/A

Ingredients:

- 1 cup fresh chopped pineapple
- 1/2 cup freshly squeezed lemon juice
- 3 cups water
- 1 cup limeade, frozen

Directions:

In a food processor, puree fresh pineapple.
Combine the pureed pineapple with the remaining ingredients and chill
for at least 1 hour.

Nutritional Information per Serving:

*Calories: 54; Total Fat: 0.6 g; Carbs: 12 g; Dietary Fiber: trace;
Protein: 0.9 g; Cholesterol: 0 mg; Sodium: 30 mg; sugars: 9.2 g*

86. The Super-Eight Detox Juice

Yield: 2 Servings
Total Time: 10 Minutes
Prep Time: 10 Minutes
Cook Time: N/A

Ingredients

- 1 cup collard greens
- 1 cup kale
- 1 cup baby spinach
- 1 green apple
- 1 carrot
- 1 red beet
- 1 cup blackberries 1 cup blueberries

Directions

Juice all ingredients and enjoy!

Nutritional Information per Serving:

Calories: 133; Total Fat: 0.9 g; Carbs: 30.7 g; Dietary Fiber: 8.9 g; Sugars: 16.3 g Protein: 4.6 g; Cholesterol: 0 mg; Sodium: 91 mg

87. Gingery Lemonade

Serving Total: 4 servings
Total Time: 12 Minutes
Prep Time: 5 Minutes Cook
Time: 7 Minutes

Ingredients:

- 14 slices fresh ginger root
- 4 quarts water
- 1 tablespoon raw honey
- 4 cups fresh lemon juice 2
- lemons, sliced

Directions:

Combine ginger root, water and honey in a saucepan set over medium heat; bring to a gentle boil. Remove from heat and stir in lemon juice. Let cool for about 15 minutes and chill for at least 1 hour. Serve over ice garnished with lemon slices.

Nutritional Information per Serving:

Calories: 98; Total Fat: 2.1 g; Carbs: 10.2 g; Dietary Fiber: 1.1 g; Protein: 2.1 g; Cholesterol: 0 mg; Sodium: 76 mg; sugars: 9.4 g

88. Turmeric Ginger Fenugreek Latte

Yield: 1 Serving
Total Time: 5 Minutes
Prep Time: 5 Minutes
Cook Time: 5 Minutes

Ingredients

- 1 cup skim milk
- 1 tablespoon fenugreek powder
- 1 teaspoon raw honey
- 1 teaspoon fresh lemon zest
- 1 teaspoon cinnamon
- 1 teaspoon ginger powder 1
  teaspoon turmeric

Directions

Heat skim milk until hot; remove from heat and whisk un the remaining ingredients until very smooth and frothy. Enjoy!

Nutritional Information per Serving:

Calories: 197; Total Fat: 12 g; Carbs: 6 g; Dietary Fiber: 4 g; Sugar: 1 g; Protein: 0 g; Cholesterol: 13 mg; Sodium: 131 mg

89. Slimming Lemon Detox Water

Yield: 2 Servings
Total Time: 5 Minutes
Prep Time: 5 Minutes
Cook Time: N/A

Ingredients

- 1/2 cucumber, sliced
- 3 slices fresh ginger, peeled
- 1 lemon, sliced
- 1 lime, sliced
- 1 orange, sliced
- 1 cup chopped mint leaves
- 1   cup ice
- 2   cup water

Directions

in a large jug, layer ice and all the ingredients; top with water and let the flavors blend for at least 30 minutes before drinking.

Nutritional Information per Serving:

Calories: 19; Total Fat: 0 g; Carbs: 5 g; Dietary Fiber: 1 g; Sugar: 2 g; Protein: 0 g; Cholesterol: 0 mg; Sodium: 2 mg

90. Lime Lemon Slush

Serving Total: 2 servings
Total Time: 5 Minutes
Prep Time: 5 Minutes Cook
Time: N/A

Ingredients:

- 2 limes
- 2 lemons
- 1/8 cup raw honey
- 1 cup pure water Ice
-

Directions:

Blend everything in a blender until smooth. Enjoy!

Nutritional Information per Serving:

Calories: 64; Total Fat: 0 g; Carbs: 17.5 g; Dietary Fiber: trace; Protein: 2.1 g; Cholesterol: 0 mg; Sodium: 2 mg; sugars: 17.4 g

91. Slimming Smoothie

Serving Total: 4 servings
Total Time: 5 Minutes
Prep Time: 5 Minutes Cook
Time: N/A

Ingredients:

- 1 ripe avocado
- 1/4 cantaloupe, juiced
- 1 peeled kiwi fruit, juiced

Directions:

Combine the juice and avocado in a blender and blend until smooth.

Nutritional Information per Serving:

Calories: 117; Total Fat: 9.9 g; Carbs: 7.8 g; Dietary Fiber: 4 g; Protein: 1.2 g; Cholesterol: 0 mg; Sodium: 5 mg; sugars: 2.6 g

92. Gingery Grape Juice

Serving Total: 1 servings
Total Time: 5 Minutes
Prep Time: 5 Minutes Cook
Time: N/A

Ingredients:

- 2 cups red grapes
- 1 2-inch peeled ginger
- 1 medium lemon, peeled, juiced 4 oz.
- water

Directions:

Combine all ingredients in a blender; blend until very smooth. Enjoy!

Nutritional Information per Serving:

Calories: 159; Total Fat: 1.1 g; Carbs: 40.8 g; Dietary Fiber: 4 g; Protein: 2.3 g; Cholesterol: 0 mg; Sodium: 10 mg; sugars: 31.5 g

93. Fat-Burner Juice

Yield: 3 Servings
Total Time: 10 Minutes
Prep Time: 10 Minutes
Cook Time: N/A

Ingredients

- 1 	cup of choice greens
- 2 	celery stalks
- 2 green apples
- 2 carrots
- 1 red sweet pepper
- 1 peeled lemon 1 ginger

Directions

Juice everything together. Enjoy!

Nutritional Information per Serving:

Calories: 57; Total Fat: 0.2 g; Carbs: 10.7 g; Dietary Fiber: 3.9 g; Protein: 1.7 g; Cholesterol: 0 mg; Sodium: 25 mg; sugars: 8.4 g

94. Garlicky Green Juice

Yield: 2 Servings
Total Time: 10 Minutes
Prep Time: 10 Minutes
Cook Time: N/A

Ingredients

- 1 green apple
- 1 cup kale
- 1 celery stalk
- 1 clove garlic Ginger

Directions

Juice everything together. Enjoy!

Nutritional Information per Serving:

Calories: 67; Total Fat: 0.2 g; Carbs: 16.8 g; Dietary Fiber: 2.9 g; Protein: 1.2 g; Cholesterol: 0 mg; Sodium: 22 mg; sugars: 9.6 g

95. The Super-8 Detox Juice

Yield: 2 Servings
Total Time: 10 Minutes
Prep Time: 10 Minutes
Cook Time: N/A

Ingredients

- 1 collard leaf
- 1 kale leaf
- 1 broccoli floret
- 1 tomato
- 1/2 red pepper
- 1 carrot
- 1 stalk of celery
  Handful of parsley

Directions

Juice all ingredients and enjoy!

Nutritional Information per Serving:

Calories: 66; Total Fat: 0.4 g; Carbs: 13.8 g; Dietary Fiber: 4.2 g; Protein: 3.6 g; Cholesterol: 0 mg; Sodium: 64 mg; sugars: 4.5 g

96. Kale-Beetroot Juice

Total Time: 5 Minutes
Prep Time: 5 Minutes
Cook Time: N/A

Ingredients

- 2 leaves of Kale
- 1   apple, cored
- 2   carrots, chopped
- 1 stalk of celery, chopped
- 1 small beetroot, chopped

Directions

Combine all the ingredients together in a blender and blend until smooth.

Nutritional Information per Serving:

Calories: 201; Total Fat: 0.5 g; Carbs: 49.6 g; Dietary Fiber: 9.9 g; Protein: 4 g; Cholesterol: 0 mg; Sodium: 179 mg; sugars: 31.9 g

Yield: 1 Serving

97. Gingery Pineapple Paradise

Yield: 2 Servings
Total Time: 5 Minutes
Prep Time: 5 Minutes
Cook Time: N/A

Ingredients

- 1-inch piece fresh ginger
- 1/2 cup pineapple chunks
- 2 tablespoons lime juice
- 1 apple, diced
- 1/2 cup mango chunks

Directions

Blend together all ingredients until smooth. Serve over ice.

Nutritional Information per Serving:

Calories: 186; Total Fat: 0.8 g; Carbs: 47.2 g; Dietary Fiber: 6.6 g; Protein: 1.8 g; Cholesterol: 0 mg; Sodium: 6 mg; sugars: 28.7 g

98. Citrus Drink

Total Time: 10 Minutes
Prep Time: 10 Minutes
Cook Time: N/A

Ingredients

- 1 large grapefruit
- 1   orange   1
- lemon

Directions

Juice red grapefruit and orange; set aside. Squeeze in the lemon juice and stir to combine well.

Nutritional Information per Serving:

Calories: 193; Total Fat: 0.6 g; Carbs: 48.6g; Dietary Fiber: 8.1g; Protein: 3.8g; Cholesterol: 0mg; Sodium: 0mg; sugars: 40.4g

Yield: 1 Serving

Total Time: 5 Minutes
Prep Time: 5 Minutes
Cook Time: N/A

Ingredients

- ¼ cup fresh lemon juice 1 cup
- hot water
- 1 teaspoon raw honey
- ¼ teaspoon cayenne pepper
- 1/8 teaspoon ground ginger 1/8
- teaspoon turmeric

Directions

In a mug, stir everything together until well blended. Enjoy!

Nutritional Information per Serving:

Yield: 1 Serving
Calories: 39; Total Fat: 0.6 g; Carbs: 7.6 g; Dietary Fiber: 0.5 g; Sugars: 7.1 g; Protein: 0.6 g; Cholesterol: 0 mg; Sodium: 20 mg

100. Super Detox Drink

Total Time: 5 Minutes
Prep Time: 5 Minutes Cook
Time: N/A

Ingredients:

- 1 cup warm water
- 1 teaspoon raw honey
- 1   dash cayenne pepper
- ¼ teaspoon cinnamon
- 2   tablespoon apple cider vinegar
- ½-1 teaspoon ground ginger 2 tablespoon lemon juice

Directions:

In a jug, mix all the ingredients together until well combined. Serve over ice.

Yield: 1 Serving
Nutritional Information per Serving:

Calories: 40; Total Fat: 0.3 g; Carbs: 7.9 g; Dietary Fiber: 0.6 g; Sugars: 6.6 g; Protein: 0.4 g; Cholesterol: 0 mg; Sodium: 15 mg

Yield: 1 Serving

HOW TO INTERMITTENT FAST

TYPE OF INTERMITTENT FASTING	DURATION OF FASTING PERIOD	DESCRIPTION
Time-restricted eating (TRE)	12-16 hours every day	Restricting daily food consumption to a 4- to 12-hour window
Alternate-day fasting	24-hours every other day	Alternating days (24-hour periods) of fasting with eating as much as desired (1:1 day eating-fasting cycle)
5:2 intermittent fasting	2 days every week	Fasting each week for two days followed by five days of eating as much as desired (5:2 day eating-fasting cycle)
Periodic fasting	48+ hours every several months	Periodic fasts lasting at least 2-3 days, often done several times a year
Fasting-mimicking diet (FMD)	3-5 days one to a few times a year	Short-term (about 3-5 days) reduction of calorie intake by at least ~50% before returning to normal eating

Yield: 1 Serving

10 benefits of intermittent fasting

1 protect against neurodegenrative diseases

2 insulin levels drop and human grown hormone increases

3 reduce unsulin resistance and lower blood sugar levels

4 reduce risk of heart disease

5 reduce blood pressure and cholesterol levels

6 boost metabolism for fat loss

7 extend lifespan, helping you live longer

8 reduce oxidative damage and inflammation in the body.

9 removes waste material from cells

10 reduce leptin levels, increasing testosterone